Cambridge BEC Preliminary 1

REGENT'S
UNIVERSITY LONDON

REGENT'S
UNIVERSITY LONDON
WITHDRAWN

Examination papers from University of Cambridge ESOL Examinations: English for Speakers of Other Languages

CAMBRIDGE
UNIVERSITY PRESS

REGENTS COLLEGE LIBRARY

17018703

CAMBRIDGE UNIVERSITY PRESS
Cambridge, New York, Melbourne, Madrid, Cape Town, Singapore,
São Paulo, Delhi, Dubai, Tokyo

Cambridge University Press
The Edinburgh Building, Cambridge CB2 8RU, UK

www.cambridge.org
Information on this title: www.cambridge.org/9780521753012

© Cambridge University Press 2002

It is normally nescessary for written permission for copying to be obtained *in advance* from a publisher. The normal requirements are waived here and it is not necessary to write to Cambridge University Press for permission for an individual teacher to make copies for use within his or her own classroom. Only those pages which carry the wording ' Photocopiable © UCLES' may be copied.

First published 2002
7th printing 2010

Printed in the United Kingdom at the University Press, Cambridge

A catalogue record for this publication is available from the British Library

ISBN 978-0-521-75301-2 Paperback
ISBN 978-0-521-75302-9 Audio Cassette
ISBN 978-0-521-75303-6 Audio CD

Cambridge University Press has no responsibility for the persistence or accuracy of URLs for external or third-party internet websites referred to in this publication, and does not guarantee that any content on such websites is, or will remain, accurate or appropriate. Information regarding prices, travel timetables and other factual information given in this work are correct at the time of first printing but Cambridge University Press does not guarantee the accuracy of such information thereafter.

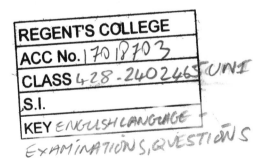

REGENT'S COLLEGE
ACC No. 170 18703
CLASS 428.2402465 UNI
S.I.
KEY ENGLISH LANGUAGE
EXAMINATIONS, QUESTIONS

Contents

Thanks and acknowledgements   iv

Introduction   1

Test 1   Reading and writing   17
Listening   31
Speaking   37

Test 2   Reading and writing   39
Listening   53
Speaking   59

Test 3   Reading and writing   61
Listening   75
Speaking   81

Test 4   Reading and writing   83
Listening   97
Speaking   103

Key (including tapescripts and model answers)
Test 1   105
Test 2   109
Test 3   114
Test 4   118

Speaking Test Interlocutor Frames   123

Sample OMR Answer Sheets   125

Thanks and acknowledgements

The authors and publishers are grateful to the following copyright owners for permission to reproduce copyright material. Every endeavour has been made to contact holders and apologies are expressed for any omissions.

p. 44 Reproduced by kind permission of the Cambridge Evening News; pp. 46 and 90 © Telegraph Group Limited 2000; p. 66 © John-Paul Flintoff; p. 70 © Manchester Evening News Syndication; p. 92 by Philip Inman © The Guardian 9.1.99

Introduction

TO THE STUDENT

This book is for candidates preparing for the University of Cambridge Local Examinations Syndicate (UCLES) Business English Certificate Preliminary Level examination. It contains four complete tests which reflect the most recent specifications (introduced in March 2002).

The BEC Suite

The Business English Certificates (BEC) are certificated examinations which can be taken on up to six fixed dates per year at approved Cambridge BEC centres. They are aimed primarily at individual learners who wish to obtain a business-related English language qualification and provide an ideal focus for courses in Business English. Set in a business context, BEC tests English language, not business knowledge. BEC is available at three levels – Preliminary, Vantage and Higher.

BEC Preliminary

Within the three levels, BEC Preliminary is at Cambridge Level 2.

| Cambridge Level 4
BEC Higher |
| Cambridge Level 3
BEC Vantage |
| Cambridge Level 2
BEC Preliminary |

The exam is based on the former Business English Certificate 1, which has been revised to keep pace with changes in business practice and language teaching and testing, and renamed.

The BEC Preliminary examination consists of three papers:

Reading and Writing	1 hour 30 minutes
Listening	40 minutes (approximately)
Speaking	12 minutes

Test of Reading and Writing (1 hour 30 minutes)

The **Reading** section of the Reading and Writing paper consists of seven parts with 45 questions, which take the form of two multiple matching tasks, four multiple choice tasks, and a form-filling or note completion task. Part 1 contains five very short texts, Part 2 contains one short text and Part 3 contains graphs, charts or tables. Parts 4, 5 and 6 each contain one longer text. Part 7 contains two short texts. The texts are mainly taken from newspapers, business magazines, business correspondence, books, leaflets, brochures, etc. They are all business related, and are selected to test a wide range of reading skills and strategies.

For the **Writing** section of the Reading and Writing paper, candidates are required to produce two pieces of Writing. For Part 1, they write a note, message, memo or email to a colleague or colleagues within the company. For Part 2, they write a piece of business correspondence to somebody outside the company.

Candidates are asked to write 30 to 40 words for Part 1 and 60 to 80 words for Part 2. For Part 1, assessment is based on achievement of task. For Part 2, assessment is based on achievement of task, range and accuracy of vocabulary and grammatical structures, organisation, content and appropriacy of register and format.

Test of Listening (approximately 40 minutes)

This paper consists of four parts with 30 questions, which take the form of two multiple choice tasks and two note completion tasks. Part 1 contains eight very short conversations or monologues, Part 2 contains a short conversation or monologue, Part 3 contains a monologue, and Part 4 contains one longer text. The texts are audio-recordings based on a variety of sources including interviews, telephone calls, face to face conversations and documentary features. They are all business related, and are selected to test a wide range of listening skills and strategies.

Test of Speaking (12 minutes)

The Speaking Test consists of three parts, which take the form of an interview section, a short talk on a business topic, and a discussion. Candidates are examined in pairs by two examiners, an Interlocutor and an Assessor. The Assessor awards a mark based on the following four criteria: Grammar and Vocabulary, Discourse Management, Pronunciation and Interactive Communication. The Interlocutor provides a global mark for the whole test.

Marks and results

The three BEC Preliminary papers total 120 marks, after weighting. Each skill (Reading, Writing, Listening and Speaking) is weighted to 30 marks. A candidate's overall grade is based on the total score gained in all three papers. It is not necessary to achieve a satisfactory level in all three papers in order to pass the examination. Pass grades are Pass with Merit and Pass, with Pass with Merit being the higher. Narrow Fail and Fail are failing grades. Every candidate is provided with a Statement of Results which includes a graphical display of their performance in each skill. These are shown against the scale Exceptional – Good – Borderline – Weak and indicate the candidate's relative performance in each paper.

TO THE TEACHER

Candidature

Each year BEC is taken by over 50,000 candidates throughout the world. Most candidates are either already in work or studying in preparation for the world of work.

Content, preparation and assessment

Material used throughout BEC is as far as possible authentic and free of bias, and reflects the international flavour of the examination. The subject matter should not advantage or disadvantage certain groups of candidates, nor should it offend in areas such as religion, politics or sex.

TEST OF READING

PART	MAIN SKILL FOCUS	Input: Text type, content	Response	No. of Items /marks
1	Reading – understanding short, real world notices, messages, etc.	Notices, messages, timetables, adverts, leaflets, etc.	Multiple choice	5
2	Reading – detailed comprehension of factual material; skimming and scanning skills	Notice, list, plan, contents page, etc.	Matching	5
3	Reading – interpreting visual information	Graphs, charts, tables. etc. (The information may be presented in 8 separate graphics or combined into a single graphic.)	Matching	5
4	Reading for detailed factual information	Longer text (approx. 150–200 words): advert, business letter, product description, report, minutes, etc.	Right/Wrong/ Doesn't say	7
5	Reading for gist and specific information	Longer text (approx. 300–400 words): newspaper or magazine article, advert, report, leaflet, etc.	Multiple choice	6
6	Reading – grammatical accuracy and understanding of text structure	Longer text (approx. 125–150 words): newspaper or magazine article, advert, leaflet, etc.	Multiple choice cloze	12
7	Reading and information transfer	Short memos, letters, notices, adverts, etc.	Form-filling, note completion	5

Reading Part One

In this part there are five short texts, each of which is accompanied by a multiple choice question containing three options. In all cases the information will be brief and clear and the difficulty of the task will not lie in understanding context but in identifying or interpreting meaning.

A wide variety of text types, representative of the world of international business, can appear in this part. Each text will be complete and have a recognisable context.

Preparation
In order to prepare for this part it would be useful to expose students to a wide range of notices and short texts taken from business settings. It is also useful to practise answering sample questions, asking students to explain why the answer is correct (and why the two incorrect options do not apply).

Reading Part Two

This is a matching task comprising one text and five questions, which are often descriptions of people's requirements. Candidates are required to match each question to an appropriate part of the text labelled A–H. (As there are only five questions, some of the labels are redundant.) The testing focus of this part is vocabulary and meaning.

Preparation
For preparation purposes, students need to be familiar with text types that are divided into lists, headings or categories; for example, the contents page of a directory or book, the plan of an office, the departments in a business or shop, the items in a catalogue, etc. Many of the questions in this part require a simple interpretation of what the parts of the text mean and preparation for this could involve setting students real-world tasks of this kind using authentic (but simple) sources.

Reading Part Three

This task consists of eight graphs or charts (or a single chart or graph with 8 distinct elements) and five questions. Each question is a description of a particular visual and candidates are expected to match the questions to their corresponding graphs which are labelled A–H.

Preparation
This part focuses on understanding trends and changes. Candidates need to be able to interpret graphic data and understand the language used to describe it. Expressions such as 'rose steadily', 'remained stable', 'decreased slowly', 'reached a peak' should be introduced to students, along with relevant topics, such as sales of goods, share price movement and monthly costs.

Reading Part Four

This task is a text accompanied by seven, three-option multiple choice items. Each question presents a statement and candidates are expected to indicate whether the statement is A 'Right' or B 'Wrong' according to the text, or whether the information is not given in the text (C 'Doesn't say'). Candidates will not be expected to understand every word in the text but they should be able to pick out salient points and infer meaning where words in the text are unfamiliar. The questions will refer to factual information in the text but candidates will be required to do some processing in order to answer the questions correctly.

Preparation
This can be a difficult task for candidates who are not familiar with the three choices represented by A, B and C, and who might not understand the difference between a statement that is incorrect and one that depends on information that is not provided in the text. Students need to be trained to identify a false statement which means that the opposite or a contradictory statement is made in the text and to recognise that this is not the same as a statement that is not sufficiently covered in the text (for which an alternative answer might be 'Don't know').

Reading Part Five

This part presents a single text accompanied by six multiple choice comprehension items. The text is informative and is often taken from a leaflet, or from a newspaper or magazine article.

Candidates are expected to employ more complex reading strategies in this task, in that they should demonstrate their ability to extract relevant information, to read for gist and detail, to scan the text for specific information, and to understand the purpose of the writer and the audience for which the text is intended.

Preparation
In preparing candidates for this part, it would be a good idea to expose them to a variety of texts of a similar length. As texts become longer, slow readers are at a disadvantage and some practice in improving reading speed would be beneficial for this part. It would also be useful to discuss the following areas:
- the title
- the topic
- the writer's purpose
- the theme or main idea of each paragraph
- factual details that can be found in the text
- the writer's opinions (if they are evident)

Reading Part Six

This is a multiple choice cloze test. Candidates have to select the correct word from three options to complete twelve gaps. This part has a predominantly grammatical focus and tests candidates' understanding of the general and detailed meaning of a text and in particular their ability to analyse structural patterns.

Preparation

Any practice in the grammatical and structural aspects of the language is useful in preparing students for this part. However, it is equally important for students to analyse the structure and coherence of language within longer discourse so that they are encouraged to read for meaning beyond the sentence level. As tasks such as this typically focus on common grammatical difficulties, it is also useful to ask students to analyse the errors in their own work. Pairwork activities might be productive as students can often help each other in the areas of error identification and analysis.

Reading Part Seven

Candidates are given two short texts, for example a memo and an advertisement, and are asked to complete a form based on this material. There are five gaps, which should be completed with a word, a number or a short phrase. In this part, candidates are tested on their ability to extract relevant information and complete a form accurately.

For this part, candidates need to transfer their answers in capital letters to an Answer Sheet.

Marks

One mark is given for each correct answer. The total score for Reading is then weighted to 30 marks.

TEST OF WRITING

PART	Functions/Communicative Task	Input	Response	Register
1	e.g. (re-) arranging appointments, asking for permission, giving instructions	Rubric only (plus layout of output text type)	Internal communication (medium may be note or message or memo or email) (30–40 words)	Neutral/informal
2	e.g. apologising and offering compensation, making or altering reservations, dealing with requests, giving information about a product	One piece of input which may be business correspondence (medium may be letter, fax or email), internal communication (medium may be note, memo or email) notice, advert, etc. (plus layout or output text type, unless a letter)	Business correspondence (medium may be letter or fax or email) (60–80 words)	Neutral/formal

For BEC Preliminary, candidates are required to produce two pieces of Writing:
- an internal company communication; this means a piece of communication with a colleague or colleagues within the company on a business-related matter, and the delivery medium may be a note, message, memo or email;

- a piece of business correspondence; this means correspondence with somebody outside the company (e.g. a customer or supplier) on a business-related matter, and the delivery medium may be letter, fax or email.

Writing Part One

Candidates are asked to produce a concise piece of internal company communication of between 30 and 40 words, using a written prompt. The text will need to be produced in the form of a note, message, memo or email, and candidates are given guidance on the layout of memos and emails. The reason for writing and target reader are specified in the rubric and bullet points explain what content points have to be included. Relevant ideas for one or more of these points will have to be 'invented' by the candidate.

Writing Part Two

Candidates are asked to produce an extended piece of business correspondence of between 60 and 80 words. This task involves the processing of a short text, such as a letter or advertisement, in order to respond to it. A number of bulleted content points below the text clearly indicate what should be included in the answer. Some of this information will need to be 'invented' by the candidate.

Although the use of some key words is inevitable, candidates should not 'lift' phrases from the question paper to use in their answers. This may be penalised.

Preparing for the Writing questions

In preparing students for the Writing tasks it would be beneficial to familiarise them with a variety of business correspondence. Analysing authentic correspondence would help students understand better how to structure their answer and the type of language to use. When doing this, it would be useful to focus on the following areas:
- the purpose of the correspondence
- references to previous communication
- factual details
- the feelings and attitude of the writer
- the level of formality
- the opening sentence
- the closing sentence
- paragraphing
- the desired outcome.

If students are in a class, it might be possible to ask them to write and reply to each other's correspondence so that they can appreciate the importance of accurate content.

In a similar fashion, internal company memos and messages might also be written and analysed in terms of the above so that students can recognise the different levels of formality involved. It is a necessary part of preparing for the test that students understand the uses of, and styles inherent in, different types of business communication so that they are aware of how and why different types of correspondence are used.

Assessment

An impression mark is awarded to each piece of writing using a general mark scheme.

For Part 1, examiners use band descriptors to assess task achievement. Each piece of writing is assigned to a band between 0 and 5.

For Part 2, examiners use band descriptors to assess language and task achievement. Each piece of writing is assigned to a band between 0 and 5 and can be awarded one of two performance levels within that band.

Acceptable performance at BEC Preliminary level is represented by Band 3.

The general impression mark schemes are used in conjunction with task-specific mark schemes which focus on criteria specific to each particular task.

American spelling and usage is acceptable.

The band scores awarded are translated to a mark out of 5 for Part 1 and a mark out of 10 for Part 2. The total score for Writing is then weighted to 30 marks.

General mark scheme for Writing Part 1

	Mark
Very good attempt at task, achieving all content points. *Minimal effort is required by the reader.*	5
Good attempt at task, achieving all content points. *Some effort may be required by the reader.*	4
Satisfactory attempt at task, achieving 2 content points.	3
Inadequate attempt achieving 1 content point and/or with noticeable omissions or irrelevance.	2
Poor attempt at task; no content points achieved, has little relevance; task possibly misunderstood.	1
No relevant response or too little language to assess.	0

General mark scheme for Writing Part 2

Band		Mark
5	Full realisation of the task set. • All four content points achieved. • Confident and ambitious use of language; errors are minor, due to ambition and non-impeding. • Good range of structure and vocabulary. • Effectively organised, with appropriate use of simple linking devices. • Register and format consistently appropriate. Very positive effect on the reader.	9 or 10
4	Good realisation of the task set. • Three or four content points achieved. • Ambitious use of language; some non-impeding errors. • More than adequate range of structure and vocabulary. • Generally well-organised, with attention paid to cohesion. • Register and format on the whole appropriate. Positive effect on the reader.	7 or 8
3	Reasonable achievement of the task set. • Three content points achieved. • A number of errors may be present, but are mostly non-impeding. • Adequate range of structure and vocabulary. • Organisation and cohesion is satisfactory, on the whole. • Register and format reasonable, although not entirely successful. Satisfactory effect on the reader.	5 or 6
2	Inadequate attempt at the task set. • Two or three content points achieved. • Numerous errors, which sometimes impede communication. • Limited range of structure and vocabulary. • Content is not clearly organised or linked, causing some confusion. • Inappropriate register and format. Negative effect on the reader.	3 or 4
1	Poor attempt at the task set. • One or two content points achieved. • Serious lack of control; frequent basic errors. • Little evidence of structure and vocabulary required by task. • Lack of organisation, causing a breakdown in communication. • Little attempt at appropriate register and format. Very negative effect on the reader.	1 or 2
0	Achieves nothing. Either fewer than 25% of the required number of words or totally illegible or totally irrelevant.	0

TEST OF LISTENING

PART	MAIN SKILL FOCUS	Input	Item type	No. of Items
1	Listening for specific information	Short conversations/ monologues (40–60 words)	3-option multiple choice	8
2	Listening for specific information	Short telephone conversation/ prompted monologue (200 words)	Gap filling (numbers and spellings)	7
3	Listening for specific information	Monologue (320 words)	Note-taking (content words inc. one date)	7
4	Listening for gist/specific information	Conversation/Interview/ Discussion 2 (or 3) speakers (600 words)	3-option multiple choice Stems can be questions or stem completion	8

Listening Part One

The eight questions in this part of the paper are three-option multiple choice questions. For each question, candidates hear a short conversation or monologue, typically lasting around 15 to 30 seconds. Each monologue or dialogue is repeated on the tape in order to give candidates a chance to check their answer. The multiple choice options may be textual or they may be in the form of pictures, graphs or diagrams.

In the extracts in Part One candidates are being tested on their understanding of spoken English used in a range of situations and on their ability to extract factual information. They may need to pick out a name or time or place.

Alternatively, they may have to identify a trend in a graph or a place on a map or the location of an object in a room. In every case it will be necessary for candidates to follow the conversation closely.

Listening Part Two

This part consists of a short conversation or monologue, typically lasting around a minute and a half, which contains factual information. On the question paper there is a form, table, chart or set of notes with seven gaps where information is missing. Candidates have to complete each of the gaps. This part has a numerical focus and the answers may include dates, prices, percentages or figures.

Listening Part Three

Candidates hear a monologue. On the question paper there is a set of notes or a form with gaps. There are seven gaps to complete and the answers may be one or two words.

Listening Part Four

This part, which lasts about three minutes, contains a longer listening text which generally takes the form of an interview, or a discussion between two or possibly more speakers. There are eight, three-option multiple choice questions on the question paper and these are always in a written format. In this part of the Listening component candidates are being tested on their ability to understand the gist of a longer text and extract detailed and specific information as required by the questions. They may also be tested on the speakers' opinions.

At the end of the Listening Test, candidates have ten minutes to transfer their answers to their Answer Sheet.

Preparing for the Listening Paper

The Listening component is carefully paced and candidates are tested on short extracts in Part One so that they can gradually 'tune in' to the spoken language and improve their listening skills without losing their place in the test.

Listening can be a very demanding activity and candidates should practise their listening skills regularly using a wide variety of listening sources. Candidates who enter the Listening test having done this will be at an advantage.

At BEC Preliminary level, it is advisable to collect as much listening material as possible that is suitably paced and of an appropriate length. Native speakers speak at many different speeds and some speak much more clearly than others. If it is possible to collect a bank of authentic material that is carefully chosen, this would prove useful practice for students. Otherwise it might be better to make use of specially designed materials for this level.

For Part One, candidates should try to listen to short extracts of speech concentrating on understanding the general idea or main points of what is said. For Parts Two and Three, practice should be given in note-taking. Prior to hearing tapes or audio materials, students should be given details of the information they need to listen for. Teachers should discuss the task with the students beforehand and encourage them to listen for clues and prompts that will help them identify the points they need to find. When listening to longer texts, it would also be useful to discuss areas such as:
- the purpose of the speech or conversation
- the speakers' roles
- the speakers' opinions
- the language functions being used
- factual details
- conclusions.

Marks

One mark is given for each correct answer, giving a total score of 30 marks for the whole Listening paper.

TEST OF SPEAKING

PART	Format and Focus	Time	Candidate Focus
1	Conversation between the interlocutor and each candidate General interaction and social language	About 2 minutes	The interlocutor encourages the candidates to give information about themselves and to express personal opinions
2	A 'mini presentation' by each candidate on a business theme Organising a larger unit of discourse Giving information and expressing opinions	About 5 minutes	The candidates are given prompts which generate a short talk on a business-related topic
3	Two-way conversation between candidates followed by further prompting from the interlocutor. Expressing opinions, agreeing and disagreeing	About 5 minutes	The candidates are presented with a scenario supported by visual or written prompts which generates a discussion The interlocutor extends the discussion with further spoken prompts

Speaking Part One

In the first part of the test, the interlocutor addresses each candidate in turn and asks questions about where they work or study, where they live or what they do in their free time. The questions will be slightly different for each candidate and candidates will not be addressed in strict sequence. This part of the test lasts about two minutes and during this time, candidates are being tested on their ability to talk about themselves; to provide information on subjects such as their home, hobbies and jobs, and to perform simple functions such as agreeing and disagreeing and expressing preferences.

Speaking Part Two

The second part of the test is a 'mini presentation'. Candidates are asked to speak for about one minute on a business related topic. At Preliminary level candidates are given two topics from which they should choose **one**. Each topic is presented as a main focus with three bullet points. Candidates may choose to expand on some or all of the bullet points but should be aware of the need to speak for at least 45 seconds. Candidates are given one minute to prepare the talk (both candidates or group of three prepare at the same time). After each candidate finishes speaking the next candidate is asked a question related to the talk. This part of the test focuses on the candidate's ability to present basic ideas and organise a longer piece of discourse.

Speaking Part Three

The third part of the test is a two-way conversation (three-way in a three candidate format) between candidates. The interlocutor outlines a scenario and provides prompts by way of black and white pictures or written prompts to help the candidates. The candidates are asked to speak for about two minutes. The interlocutor will support the conversation as appropriate and then ask further questions related to the main theme. This part of the test focuses on the candidate's ability to interact appropriately using a range of linguistic skills.

Preparing for the Speaking test

It is important to familiarise candidates with the format of the test before it takes place, by the use of paired activities in class. Teachers may need to explain the benefits of this type of assessment to candidates. The primary purpose of paired assessment is to sample a wider range of discourse than can be elicited from an individual interview.

In the first part of the test, candidates mainly respond to questions or comments from the interlocutor. In the second part candidates are given the opportunity to produce an extended piece of discourse and to demonstrate an ability to maintain a longer piece of speech. In the third part they are required to interact more actively, taking turns appropriately, asking and answering questions and negotiating meaning. To prepare for this part, it is a good idea to encourage students to change partners in class so that they grow accustomed to interacting with a variety of people, some of whom they do not know well.

For all parts of the test students need to practise the exchange of personal and non-personal information and prompt materials will be needed to help them do this. Teachers could prepare a selection of these for each part of the test. Students could discuss the materials as a class group prior to engaging in pairwork activities. Such activities would familiarise students with the types of interactive skills involved in asking and providing factual information such as: speaking clearly, formulating questions, listening carefully and giving precise answers.

Assessment

Candidates are assessed on their own performance and not in relation to each other according to the following analytical criteria; Grammar and Vocabulary, Discourse Management, Pronunciation and Interactive Communication. These criteria are interpreted at Cambridge Level 2. Assessment is based on performance in the whole test.

Both examiners assess the candidates. The Assessor applies detailed, analytical scales, and the Interlocutor applies a global achievement scale which is based on the analytical scales. The analytical criteria are further described below:

Grammar and Vocabulary

This refers to range and accuracy as well as the appropriate use of grammatical and lexical forms. At BEC Preliminary, a range of grammar and vocabulary is needed to deal with the tasks. At this level candidates may make frequent minor errors and use some inappropriate vocabulary, but this should not obscure intended meanings.

Discourse Management

This refers to the coherence, extent and relevance of each candidate's individual performance. Contributions should be adequate to deal with the tasks. At times, candidates' utterances may be inappropriate in length and some utterances may lack coherence.

Pronunciation

This refers to the candidate's ability to produce comprehensible utterances. At BEC Preliminary, most meanings are conveyed through the appropriate use of stress, rhythm, intonation and clear individual sounds, although there may be some strain on the listener.

Interactive Communication

This refers to the candidate's ability to take an active part in the development of the discourse. At BEC Preliminary, candidates are able to take turns and sustain the interaction by initiating and responding appropriately. Hesitation may demand patience of the listener.

Global Achievement Scale

This refers to the candidate's overall performance throughout the test.

   Throughout the Speaking Test candidates are assessed on their language skills and in order to be able to make a fair and accurate assessment of each candidate's performance, the examiners must be given an adequate sample of language to assess. Candidates must, therefore, be prepared to provide full answers to the questions asked by either the Interlocutor or the other candidate, and to speak clearly and audibly. While it is the responsibility of the Interlocutor, where necessary, to manage or direct the interaction, thus ensuring that both candidates are given an equal opportunity to speak, it is the responsibility of the candidates to maintain the interaction as much as possible. Candidates who take equal turns in the interchange will utilise to best effect the amount of time available.

Grading and results

Grading takes place once all scripts have been returned to UCLES and marking is complete. This is approximately five weeks after the examination. There are two main stages: grading and awards.

Grading

The three papers total 120 marks, after weighting. Each skill represents 25% of the total marks available.

The grade boundaries (Pass with Merit, Pass, Narrow Fail and Fail) are set using the following information:

- statistics on the candidature
- statistics on the overall candidate performance
- statistics on individual items, for those parts of the examination for which this is appropriate (Reading and Listening)
- the advice of the Chief Examiners, based on the performance of candidates, and on the recommendation of examiners where this is relevant (Writing)
- comparison with statistics from previous years' examination performance and candidature.

A candidate's overall grade is based on the total score gained in all three papers. It is not necessary to achieve a satisfactory level in all three papers in order to pass the examination.

Awards

The Awarding Committee deals with all cases presented for special consideration, e.g. temporary disability, unsatisfactory examination conditions, suspected collusion, etc. The committee can decide to ask for scripts to be re-marked, to check results, to change grades, to withhold results, etc. Results may be withheld because of infringement of regulations or because further investigation is needed. Centres are notified if a candidate's results have been scrutinised by the Awarding Committee.

Results

Results are reported as two passing grades (Pass with Merit and Pass) and two failing grades (Narrow Fail and Fail). Candidates are given statements of results which, in addition to their grades, show a graphical profile of their performance on each paper. These are shown against the scale Exceptional – Good – Borderline – Weak and indicate the candidate's relative performance in each paper. Certificates are issued to passing candidates after the issue of statements of results and there is no limit on the validity of the certificate.

Further information

For more information about BEC or any other UCLES examination write to:
EFL Information
University of Cambridge Local Examinations Syndicate
1 Hills Road
Cambridge
CB1 2EU
United Kingdom

Tel: +44 1223 553355
Fax: +44 1223 460278
email: efl@ucles.org.uk
www.cambridge-efl.org.uk
In some areas, this information can also be obtained from the British Council.

Test 1

READING AND WRITING   1 hour 30 minutes

READING

PART ONE

Questions 1–5

- Look at the questions **1–5**.
- In each question, which sentence is correct?
- For each question, mark one letter (**A**, **B**, or **C**) on your Answer Sheet.

Example: 0

Don't forget -

flight BA692   6.45 pm

The plane arrives at

A   quarter to seven in the morning.
B   quarter past six in the evening.
C   quarter to seven in the evening.

The correct answer is **C**, so mark your Answer Sheet like this:

0	A B C

1

Please inform the supervisor if this
photocopier runs out of ink.

The supervisor

A   needs to know if there is no ink in the photocopier.
B   should repair the photocopier if it prints badly.
C   will tell you how to load the photocopier with ink.

17

2

All deliveries – please report to Reception immediately upon arrival for authority to unload.

Drivers should

A speak to Reception after delivering goods.
B unload vehicles at Reception.
C call in at Reception before unloading.

3

Jane,

I'd like to meet on Tuesday, but if my plane's delayed I'll see you at Friday's meeting.

John

A John has to postpone his meeting until Friday.
B John will be late for his meeting on Tuesday.
C John hopes to see Jane on Tuesday.

4

Company staff must advise Personnel of any change of home address, to keep files up to date.

A All staff must update their company files regularly.
B Staff must keep Personnel informed if they move house.
C Staff must inform Personnel of any company which changes address.

5

Insurance Direct phoned: re your call, could you return form by 28 September.

A Please ring Insurance Direct back about the form before 28 September.
B Send back the insurance form that you phoned about before 28 September.
C Insurance Direct have acknowledged receipt of your form dated 28 September.

PART TWO

Questions 6–10

- Look at the advertisement below. It shows the training courses which are offered by a company called Merton Training.
- For questions **6–10**, decide which course (**A–H**) is the most suitable for each person below to attend.
- For each question, mark the correct letter (**A–H**) on your Answer Sheet.
- Do not use any letter more than once.

MERTON TRAINING

SHORT RESIDENTIAL COURSES

A Advanced Presentation Skills

B Better Time Management

C Essential Team-Building in the Office

D Updating your Selling Skills

E Making the Most of Computers

F Improve your Confidence in Meetings

G Successful Telephoning

H Developing your Understanding of Accounts

---

6 The office manager needs to become more efficient in order to meet deadlines at work.

7 This member of staff has to make several calls a day but is not confident when ringing strangers.

8 The Information Technology Manager wants to improve the speech she has prepared for a conference next month.

9 An experienced sales executive needs to update his knowledge of finance before he starts work as Assistant Sales Manager.

10 A new member of the team needs to learn how to use the office software more efficiently.

PART THREE

Questions 11–15

- Look at the charts below. They show the income from sales and the income from advertisements in eight different newspapers over a three-month period in 2001.
- Which chart does each sentence (**11–15**) on the opposite page describe?
- For each sentence, mark one letter (**A–H**) on your Answer Sheet.
- Do not use any letter more than once.

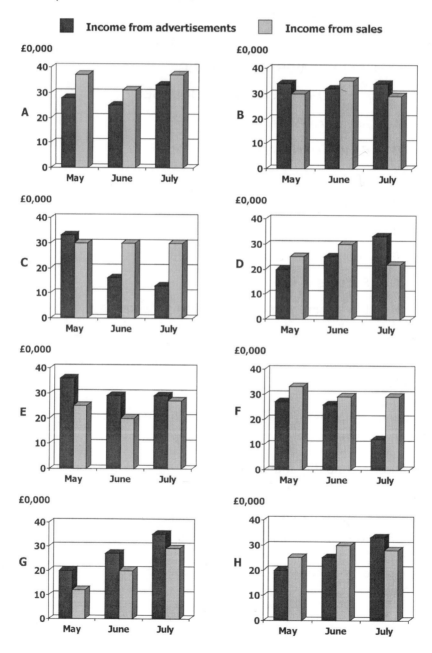

11 While income from advertisements rose steadily throughout the period, income from sales increased in June but then fell to below the May level.

12 Income from advertisements fell slightly in June and by a larger amount in July, whereas income from sales remained steady in the final month.

13 Although income from sales overtook income from advertisements in June, it then dropped back again at the end of the period.

14 Income from sales reached a low point in June while income from advertisements levelled off at the end of the period.

15 Income from advertisements reached a peak in July and income from sales was at its lowest point in June.

PART FOUR

Questions 16–22

- Read part of the letter of application below.
- Are sentences **16–22** on the opposite page 'Right' or 'Wrong'? If there is not enough information to answer 'Right' or 'Wrong', choose 'Doesn't say'.
- For each sentence **16–22**, mark one letter (**A**, **B** or **C**) on your Answer Sheet.

I would like to apply for the post of Personnel Officer with Anglia Bank, as advertised in the *Daily News* on 19 October.

I have a BA in French from the University of London. I am following a part-time course in Personnel Management at the Oxford College of Management, and I hope to pass the Diploma in Personnel Management at the end of December.

When I left university, I worked for a year in a computer company near Cambridge. Then I moved back to London to work as a French teacher in a large school, where I stayed for two years. During this time, I did some part-time work as a language trainer with factory managers, which I very much enjoyed.

Three years ago, I joined Carter's Bank, where for the past year I have worked as Assistant Personnel Officer, dealing mainly with complaints from members of staff.

Having worked in a similar organisation to yours, I feel I am fully prepared for the challenges of this job.

Yours faithfully

Angela Varley

16 Ms Varley is applying for a job with the *Daily News*.

    A Right   **B** Wrong   **C** Doesn't say

17 She obtained a Diploma in Personnel Management in December.

    A Right   **B** Wrong   **C** Doesn't say

18 She worked as a computer operator after university.

    A Right   **B** Wrong   **C** Doesn't say

19 While Ms Varley was a school teacher, she also taught company executives.

    A Right   **B** Wrong   **C** Doesn't say

20 In her present job, she has responsibility for internal personnel problems.

    A Right   **B** Wrong   **C** Doesn't say

21 She enjoys working at Carter's Bank.

    A Right   **B** Wrong   **C** Doesn't say

22 Ms Varley thinks she would be suitable for the job because of her previous experience.

    A Right   **B** Wrong   **C** Doesn't say

PART FIVE

Questions 23–28

- Read the text below about a retail group.
- For each question **23–28**, choose the correct answer.
- Mark one letter (**A**, **B** or **C**) on your Answer Sheet.

NOT JUST A SHOP!

In his yearly report, the Chairman of a chain of retail outlets writes about the financial aspects of the business and describes the work which the company has done to benefit people in the areas where their shops are located.

It continues to be an important part of our company policy to be responsible for the health and welfare of people in the areas which we serve. In the past year, we have concentrated especially on education and training, and have invested over £4,000,000 in this and other areas ranging from the care of the old to the arts.

Let us look at these first. We have, as always, financed health research and care projects helping not only the old but children and the disabled too. We were especially pleased this year to provide alarms for disabled people who live alone and to run programmes which help children understand better the problems facing disabled people.

The Groundwork Foundation encourages young people in poor areas to improve their environment, while the Schools Prom concert at the Royal Albert Hall in London includes 20,000 children nationwide. Both of these were given financial help.

As mentioned above, in the last year we have been active in supporting a range of education projects. Two of our managers are now out of the company on 1-year projects, training young people for work in the retail industry and improving the quality of the teaching they receive. In addition, we have started a programme of 3-month schemes which our managerial staff are able to benefit from without having to take a long break from their jobs.

Schools and universities have also benefited. A London Business School received £50,000 to develop a training programme for UK school staff, giving them the skills necessary to manage their own schools. A major University has received a promise of £100,000 over 5 years to fund a new teaching post in international retailing. This will allow 22 more students to study this subject each year.

It is not only the company that supports good work for other people. Members of staff themselves are encouraged to join the company Give as You Earn system, to give money to others, especially those organisations working for the benefit of the local area. In such cases the company often gives its support by making an additional contribution.

We look forward to committing even more money to these and other projects in the coming year.

23 In the past year £4,000,000 was spent on

    A   looking after old people.

    B   all the company projects.

    C   education and training.

24 This year's special help for the disabled has concentrated on

    A   improving their security.

    B   providing them with training programmes.

    C   research into their illnesses.

25 The Schools Prom concert is for children from

    A   poor parts of the country.

    B   London only.

    C   all over the country.

26 An advantage with one of the education projects is that the managers

    A   are usually good teachers.

    B   rarely leave the company.

    C   can continue their careers.

27 The company gave some financial assistance to

    A   allow more people to study at a high level.

    B   promote retailing jobs in schools.

    C   train students in schools management.

28 The company

    A   only pays into projects that the staff choose.

    B   is keen for staff to help the local community.

    C   expects staff to support only local projects.

PART SIX

Questions 29–40

- Read the advertisement below about improving keyboard skills.
- Choose the correct word to fill each gap, from **A**, **B** or **C** below.
- For each question **29–40**, mark one letter (**A**, **B** or **C**) on your Answer Sheet.

LEARN KEY SKILLS FOR YOUR COMPUTER – ON YOUR COMPUTER!

Computers are now as commonly used in business as the telephone. Therefore, it's important that people know how to use **(29)** .... efficiently. Now, you and your whole organisation are able to do this in the simplest way possible **(30)** .... learning and practising on your own, with **(31)** .... wide range of courses at beginner, intermediate and advanced level on CD-ROM.

The person **(32)** .... appears on the screen acts as your teacher, **(33)** .... you through the tasks and explaining everything. Then **(34)** .... difficult exercises allow you to practise the things you **(35)** .... learned and test your understanding.

(36) .... courses are excellent value – only £69.99. You **(37)** .... save yourself money if you buy the complete collection of seven courses. This is now available **(38)** .... the retail price of £410. You can make a further saving **(39)** .... 10% by ordering the complete collection **(40)** .... the next thirty days.

29	**A**	them	**B**	it	**C**	they
30	**A**	to	**B**	in	**C**	by
31	**A**	its	**B**	our	**C**	their
32	**A**	which	**B**	who	**C**	what
33	**A**	guide	**B**	guides	**C**	guiding
34	**A**	too	**B**	much	**C**	more
35	**A**	had	**B**	have	**C**	has

36	**A** These	**B** Each	**C** Every
37	**A** can	**B** ought	**C** need
38	**A** over	**B** at	**C** from
39	**A** with	**B** of	**C** for
40	**A** until	**B** before	**C** within

PART SEVEN

Questions 41–45

- Read the memo and the email below.
- Complete the form at the bottom of the page.
- Write a word or phrase (in CAPITAL LETTERS) or a number on lines **41–45** on your Answer Sheet.

AFT CLEANING SERVICES LTD

To: Liz Smith, Supervisor
From: Peter Broadbent, Manager

I got this email yesterday from Collins Ltd in Mill Lane. Could you fill in a new client form for them? Our new radio advertisement seems to have worked, as this is the fifth person who has contacted us!

From	Paul Tomkins [p.tomkins@collins.co.uk]
To	Peter Broadbent [p.broadbent@aftclean.com]
Sent	15 January 2002 16:46
Subject	Our telephone call on 14 January

I can confirm that we would like to employ AFT to clean our new branch at 7 Dawson Street. I'm not sure how many cleaners or what hours we will need. Please ring Sue Potts, my secretary, to arrange terms. This contract is to begin from 25 January.

NEW CLIENT DETAILS

Company:	**(41)**	....
Name of person to contact:	**(42)**	....
Address of property to be cleaned:	**(43)**	....
Starting date:	**(44)**	....
How client first heard about us:	**(45)**	....

WRITING

PART ONE

Question 46

- You have to organise an urgent meeting at 9 a.m. tomorrow with all the staff from your department.
- Write an **email** to the staff:
  - saying when the meeting will be
  - telling them where the meeting will be
  - explaining what the meeting will be about.
- Write about **30–40** words on your Answer Sheet.

PART TWO

Question 47

- Read this part of a letter from John Biggs, who is the president of a business club.

> As President of the Clifton Business Club, I would like to invite you to speak at our annual dinner on 5 July. The dinner which starts at 7.30 pm, will be held at the Mayflower Restaurant, Clifton.
>
> I hope that you are able to accept the invitation and would be grateful if you could give me the subject of your talk, so that I can include it on the invitations to our members.
>
> I look forward to receiving your reply as soon as possible.

- Write a **letter** to Mr Biggs:
  - accepting the invitation
  - telling him the subject of your talk
  - asking how long the talk should be
  - enquiring whether accommodation will be arranged for you.

- Write **60–80** words on your Answer Sheet.
- Do not include postal addresses.

LISTENING   Approximately 40 minutes (including 10 minutes' transfer time)

PART ONE

Questions 1–8

- For questions **1–8** you will hear eight short recordings.
- For each question, mark one letter (**A**, **B**, or **C**) for the correct answer.

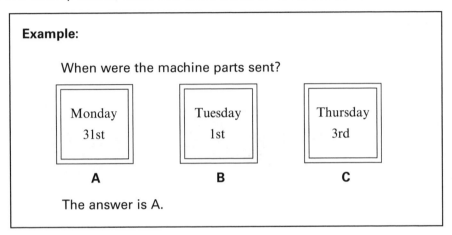

After you have listened once, replay each recording.

1   What time is the man's flight?

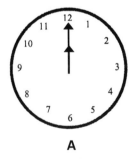

        A   **B**   **C**

2   Which is the company's new packaging design?

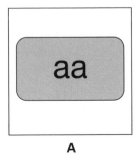

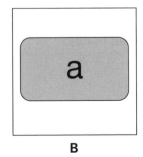

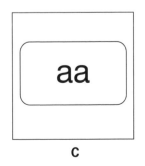

        A   **B**   **C**

3   In which part of the month were sales the highest?

   A   at the beginning
   B   in the middle
   C   at the end

4   Who does Brian Fry work for now?

   A   ANK Oil
   B   The PTI
   C   The Government

5   What is the man going to order?

A	B	C

6   What is the reduction in the company's exports?

7%	8%	9%
A	**B**	**C**

7   Where will the woman meet the visitors?

at the factory	at the office	at a restaurant
A	**B**	**C**

8   What does the woman want the man to do?

   A   call an engineer
   B   fix a machine
   C   write a sign

PART TWO

Questions 9–15

- Look at the notes below.
- Some information is missing.
- You will hear a man telephoning a company about his statement of account.
- For each question **9–15**, fill in the missing information in the numbered space using a **word**, **numbers**, or **letters**.
- After you have listened once, replay the recording.

Micro Communications Ltd
Finance Department

Name of Company: Pegasus Group

Name of Caller: **(9)**   Martin ....

Account Number: **(10)**   ....

Goods received: **(11)**   .... printers

Discount quoted originally: **(12)**   .... per cent

Correct balance due: **(13)**   £ ....

Contact number: **(14)**   840679 extension ....

Date balance will be received: **(15)**   .... October

PART THREE

Questions 16–22

- Look at the notes below.
- Some information is missing.
- You will hear Peter Dudley, Chief Executive of the Thorpe Group, giving a talk about his work to a group of business students.
- For each question **16–22**, fill in the missing information in the numbered space using **one** or **two** words.
- After you have listened once, replay the recording.

Peter Dudley
Chief Executive of the Thorpe Group

Peter Dudley's first job: **(16)** ....

At the office Peter Dudley reads: **(17)** ....

The Thorpe Group will invest more in **(18)** .... industry.

The Thorpe Group promise to customers: **(19)** ....

The Thorpe Group staff follow rules to reduce **(20)** .... for its customers.

Result of merger: company will move to **(21)** ....

The Thorpe Group recruits staff who work well in **(22)** ....

PART FOUR

Questions 23–30

- You will hear a conversation between two employees of a company which is going to move its premises.
- For each question **23–30**, mark one letter (**A**, **B** or **C**) for the correct answer.
- After you have listened once, replay the recording.

23 Who decided to move the office premises?

- **A** the company accountants
- **B** the department managers
- **C** the Board of Directors

24 Where will the new offices be?

- **A** on the edge of the city
- **B** a long way outside the city
- **C** in a different city

25 Which department will be the last to move?

- **A** Customer Services
- **B** Sales
- **C** Public Relations

26 At the new premises there will be

- **A** a staff gym.
- **B** a better staff canteen.
- **C** extra meeting rooms.

27 The company will spend most money on

- **A** special new office furniture.
- **B** new technology.
- **C** recruiting a designer.

28 What is John's main worry about the move?

- **A** the poor shopping facilities
- **B** the lack of public transport
- **C** having no other businesses near

29 The new contracts will mean that employees may

    A   have to work longer hours.
    B   only have temporary work.
    C   be able to work from home.

30 John is responsible for

    A   organising the move to new premises.
    B   giving staff general information about the move.
    C   explaining new conditions of employment.

SPEAKING   12 minutes

SAMPLE SPEAKING TASKS

PART 1

The interview – about 2 minutes

In this part the interlocutor asks questions to each of the candidates in turn. You have to give information about yourself and express personal opinions.

PART 2

'Mini presentation' – about 5 minutes

In this part of the test you are asked to give a short talk on a business topic. You have to choose one of the topics from the two below and then talk for about one minute. You have one minute to prepare your ideas.

A   WHAT IS IMPORTANT WHEN . . .?

RECRUITING NEW STAFF

- QUALIFICATIONS

- EXPERIENCE

- REFERENCES

B   WHAT IS IMPORTANT WHEN . . .?

RENTING OFFICE PREMISES

- SIZE

- LOCATION

- COST

PART 3

Discussion – about 5 minutes

The examiner reads out a scenario and gives you some prompt material in the form of pictures or words. You have 30 seconds to look at the prompt card, an example of which is below, and then about 2 minutes to discuss the scenario with your partner. After that the examiner will ask you more questions related to the topic.

For **two** or **three** candidates

Scenario

I'm going to describe a situation.

Your company is moving to another office with new furniture and equipment. Talk together about things you could put in your office and decide which 3 things would be most suitable.

Here are some ideas to help you.

Prompt material

Test 2

READING AND WRITING   1 hour 30 minutes

READING

PART ONE

Questions 1–5

- Look at the questions **1–5**.
- In each question, which sentence is correct?
- For each question, mark one letter (**A**, **B**, or **C**) on your Answer Sheet.

Example: 0

> *Don't forget -*
>
> *flight BA692   6.45 pm*

The plane arrives at

A   quarter to seven in the morning.
B   quarter past six in the evening.
C   quarter to seven in the evening.

The correct answer is **C**, so mark your Answer Sheet like this:

0	A B C

1

> Taylors rang – order for desks held up by strike.
> They expect to despatch them on 10th May.

What is the problem with the order?

A   The goods are delayed.
B   The goods are lost.
C   The goods are damaged.

2

> ## This factory will be closed until 11 am on 3 November
> ## due to essential reorganisation.

A   They will close the factory on 3 November.
B   They will move to a new factory on 3 November.
C   They will open the factory again on 3 November.

3

> **Townley Vehicles have**
> **appointed Ken Roberts,**
> **formerly of Weston Motors,**
> **as Sales Manager.**

What do we know about Ken Roberts?

A   He used to work for Townley Vehicles.
B   He is applying for a job as a sales manager.
C   He was employed by Weston Motors in the past.

4

> **EXPRESS-PRINT has opened a new office in this area.**
> **Please call in to discuss your photocopying requirements.**

A   Telephone our new office if you want to order anything.
B   Visit our new office and talk to us about what you need.
C   Contact us with your requirements when you open a new office.

5

> Sales growth at Medico plc is 1.8% this year,
> compared to an earlier forecast of 2.5%.

The company's sales growth for this year is

A   lower than expected.
B   the same as expected.
C   higher than expected.

PART TWO

Questions 6–10

- Look at the list below. It shows pages from a company's website on the internet.
- For questions **6–10**, decide which page (**A–H**) is the most suitable for each person below to select.
- For each question, mark the correct letter (**A–H**) on your Answer Sheet.
- Do not use any letter more than once.

Sky Systems Ltd: Website Directory

A	Company History
B	Company Organisation
C	Annual Report
D	Company Goals
E	Product Information
F	Retail Outlets
G	Customer Complaints
H	Latest News

---

6 Adam Smith is not satisfied with some goods he bought.

7 Rachel Cains wants to find out when the company started trading.

8 Hazel Thomas needs to know the name of the Personnel Officer.

9 Dominic Noble has to find out how the company performed last year.

10 Benjamin Tidswell wants the address of his nearest Sky Systems dealer.

PART THREE

Questions 11–15

- Look at the charts below. They show movements in the share prices of eight companies in relation to their sectors, at the close of trading on five days.
- Which chart does each sentence (**11–15**) on the opposite page describe?
- For each sentence, mark one letter (**A–H**) on your Answer Sheet.
- Do not use any letter more than once.

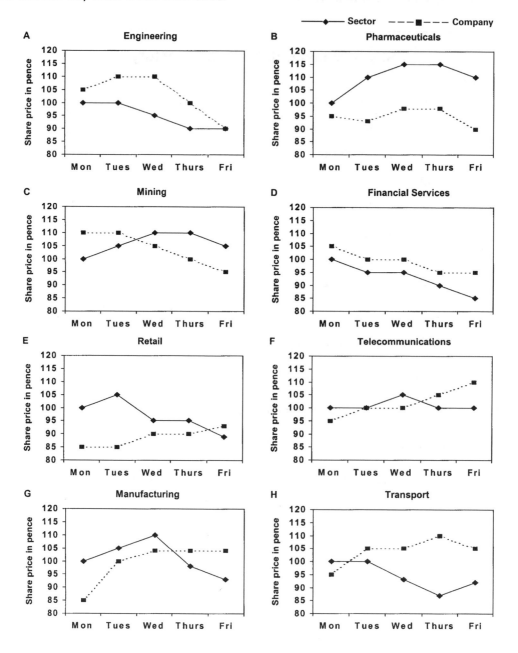

11   The sector average rose in the early part of the week, then sank back, although this company's shares remained firm after an early sharp rise.

12   This company's share price mostly kept in step with the sector average, though holding slightly firmer at the end of the week.

13   In spite of performing better than the sector average for most of the week, this company's shares lost this advantage on Friday.

14   While the sector gradually fell back, with a slight recovery at the end of the week, this company generally performed much better than the average.

15   Although there was little movement in the sector as a whole, this company's shares followed an upward trend, peaking at the end of the week.

PART FOUR

Questions 16–22

- Read the article below about a new product.
- Are sentences **16–22** on the opposite page 'Right' or 'Wrong'? If there is not enough information to answer 'Right' or 'Wrong', choose 'Doesn't say'.
- For each sentence **16–22**, mark one letter (**A**, **B** or **C**) on your Answer Sheet.

NEW PRODUCT WILL SAVE LIVES

Drinking water that looks clean may still contain bugs, which can cause illness. A small company called Genera Technologies has produced a testing method in three stages, which shows whether water is safe. The new test shows if water needs chemicals added to it, to destroy anything harmful. It was invented by scientist Dr Adrian Parton, who started Genera five years ago. He and his employees have developed the test together with a British water company.

Andy Headland, Genera's marketing director, recently presented the test at a conference in the USA and forecasts good American sales for it. Genera has already sold 11 of its tests at £42,500 a time in the UK and has a further four on order. It expects to sell another 25 tests before the end of March. The company says it is the only test in the UK to be approved by the government.

Genera was formed five years ago and until October last year had only five employees; it now employs 14. Mr Headland believes the company should make around £1.9 million by the end of the year in the UK alone.

---

16 Genera Technologies produces a product which cleans dirty water.

    A Right   **B** Wrong   **C** Doesn't say

17 Before he set up Genera, Dr Parton used to work for a British water company.

    A Right   **B** Wrong   **C** Doesn't say

18 The new product has been a commercial success in the USA.

    A Right   **B** Wrong   **C** Doesn't say

19 Each of the tests costs £42,500.

    A Right   **B** Wrong   **C** Doesn't say

20 Genera Technologies has orders for 25 more tests.

    A Right   **B** Wrong   **C** Doesn't say

21 The British government is helping Dr Parton to sell the test abroad.

    A Right   **B** Wrong   **C** Doesn't say

22 The number of employees at Genera Technologies has recently increased.

    A Right   **B** Wrong   **C** Doesn't say

PART FIVE

Questions 23–28

- Read the article below about job interviews and the questions on the opposite page.
- For each question **23–28**, on the opposite page, choose the correct answer.
- Mark one letter (**A**, **B** or **C**) on your Answer Sheet.

INTERVIEWS

People applying for jobs normally send in a copy of their CV. This should be used as a basis for questions from the interviewer.

Interviewers find it useful to ask candidates about the way they behaved in difficult situations in the past, for example with an angry customer or colleague. These questions allow applicants to explain how they acted in a real-life situation and, consequently, give clues as to how they would act again in similar situations. Candidates are likely to tell the truth as speaking from memory leaves little time to invent what happened. On the other hand questions which ask candidates to imagine how they would behave in a situation which they have probably never met are of little or no value. This is because they only provide answers about how candidates would hope to behave, and this might not match the actions they would actually take.

In any interview candidates must be treated fairly, with questions asked in the same manner and with no candidate's interview lasting considerably longer than any other's. Candidates should always be given the opportunity to ask questions throughout the interview.

Jan Godley, head of Human Resources at Aspley Supermarkets says: 'A company needs staff not only who have the right qualifications and experience, but also who are happy to fit in with the company's way of doing things. Our managers have to accept the idea that everyone working here is a colleague (managers are always known by their first names), and that spending time actually in the store with colleagues and customers, rather than in their offices, is part of the job. For management posts, we organise pre-interview group exercises to measure team-working and leadership skills, sometimes along with activities to assess personal qualities.

'In all our interviews we pay attention to body language. It is natural for candidates to show signs of being nervous at an interview but most relax after a few minutes and become more confident. However, if the nervousness continues until the end of the interview, especially when difficult questions are asked, we would begin to have doubts about that candidate. Like all employers, we want to take on staff who are at ease with colleagues and customers so it is important to watch the way candidates behave, as well as listen to what they have to say.'

23 According to the article, why are questions about a candidate's past behaviour useful?

    A   They prove the candidate will act appropriately in different circumstances.

    B   They show the candidate can remember details of the situation.

    C   They demonstrate how the candidate might act in the future.

24 Why is asking candidates to imagine their reactions to a situation unhelpful?

    A   Candidates may have no experience of this situation.

    B   Candidates may act differently in the real-life situation.

    C   Candidates may never meet such a situation.

25 According to the article,

    A   candidates should ask questions at the end of the interview.

    B   interviewers should ask all the candidates the same question.

    C   interviews should all last for roughly the same length of time.

26 What does Jan Godley say about the managers in her company?

    A   They must spend some time with customers in the store.

    B   They must know the first names of all their staff.

    C   They must spend most of their time in their offices.

27 Management applicants at Aspley Supermarkets are

    A   asked a number of questions about their personal qualities.

    B   assessed on their ability to work within a group.

    C   asked to say what leadership skills the job will require.

28 According to Jan Godley, how do candidates often behave at interviews?

    A   They show a lack of confidence at first.

    B   They are skilled at hiding their nervousness.

    C   They suddenly lose confidence when asked difficult questions.

PART SIX

Questions 29–40

- Read the magazine article below about a company which checks on the service provided by shops.
- Choose the correct word to fill each gap, from **A**, **B** or **C** on the opposite page.
- For each question **29–40**, mark one letter (**A**, **B** or **C**) on your Answer Sheet.

SECRET SHOPPERS

Tim Wright knows all about making companies more efficient. His firm, *Check-up*, sends 'secret shoppers' into retail and leisure companies (**29**) .... order to make sure that customers are receiving good service. After (**30**) .... visit, the secret shoppers prepare a report for the company to let them know (**31**) .... good or bad the service was.

'Companies like to know,' says Mr Wright, 'that (**32**) .... customers go into a store just a few minutes before closing time, they will (**33**) .... get good service.'

Check-up (**34**) .... set up in the west of England in 1992 and (**35**) .... two years moved to London so it could offer a nationwide service. (**36**) .... the last three years, *Check-up*'s profits have (**37**) .... dramatically as companies have come to realise (**38**) .... great importance of good customer service. Having started with just three employees, *Check-up* now has a staff (**39**) .... sixty-five and last week (**40**) .... an important new contract with a major supermarket chain.

29	**A** in	**B** by	**C** on
30	**A** our	**B** his	**C** their
31	**A** whether	**B** how	**C** if
32	**A** while	**B** when	**C** as
33	**A** still	**B** yet	**C** already
34	**A** has	**B** is	**C** was
35	**A** until	**B** after	**C** later
36	**A** From	**B** During	**C** Since
37	**A** increase	**B** increasing	**C** increased
38	**A** this	**B** that	**C** the
39	**A** of	**B** at	**C** too
40	**A** sign	**B** signed	**C** signing

PART SEVEN

Questions 41–45

- Read the memo and letter below.
- Complete the form at the bottom of the page.
- Write a word or phrase (in CAPITAL LETTERS) or a number on lines **41–45** on your Answer Sheet.

MEMO

To: Jo Montenegro
From: Zhara Farrell
Date: 25 February 2002
Subject: Bob Young

One of the warehouse assistants, Bob Young, has broken his arm. Here is the letter from his doctor; please let Bob's line manager know how long he will be away, and fill in a sick pay form for him.

---

24 February 2002

To whom it may concern

This is to inform you that Mr B Young has a broken arm. He should not return to work for a fortnight.

Dr Jake Parry

Employee Sick Pay Form

Name of employee:	**(41)**	....
Position	**(42)**	....
Name of doctor:	**(43)**	....
Reason for absence:	**(44)**	....
Length of absence:	**(45)**	....

WRITING

PART ONE

Question 46

- You have ordered some new office equipment. However, some of this equipment will arrive a week later than planned.
- Write a **memo** to all staff:
  - saying which equipment will be delayed
  - explaining when it will arrive
  - apologising for the delay.
- Write about **30–40** words on your Answer Sheet.

Memo

To: All Staff

From: Supplies Manager

Date: 1 March 2002

Subject: New Equipment

PART TWO

Question 47

- Read this part of a letter from the conference organiser at Greenwood Conference Centre.

> Thank you for your enquiry about conference facilities at Greenwood. I enclose a brochure containing further details of the accommodation and conference facilities which I mentioned on the phone.
>
> I am now able to confirm that Greenwood is available for up to 40 participants on the weekends of 20–22 April and 5–7 May 2001.
>
> Please do not hesitate to contact me if you require any further information.

- Write a **letter** to Mr Stanton, the conference organiser:

  - informing him which dates you would like to book
  - telling him how many participants there will be
  - giving details of the type of accommodation required
  - asking him to confirm the cost of the weekend.

- Write **60–80** words on your Answer Sheet.
- Do not include postal addresses.

LISTENING Approximately 40 minutes (including 10 minutes' transfer time)

PART ONE

Questions 1–8

- For questions **1–8** you will hear eight short recordings.
- For each question, mark one letter (**A**, **B**, or **C**) for the correct answer.

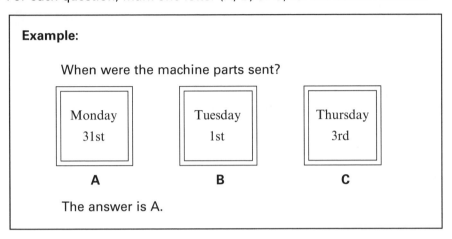

Example:

When were the machine parts sent?

Monday 31st	Tuesday 1st	Thursday 3rd
A	**B**	**C**

The answer is A.

After you have listened once, replay each recording.

1 In which month will the auditors come?

September	November	December
A	**B**	**C**

2 Which products have sold best?

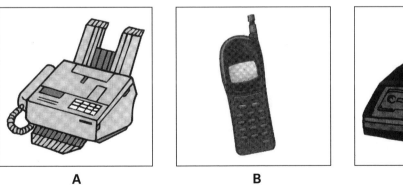

  A **B** **C**

3 Where was the flight delayed?

Sydney   Hong Kong   Singapore

   A   **B**   **C**

4 When are they going to meet?

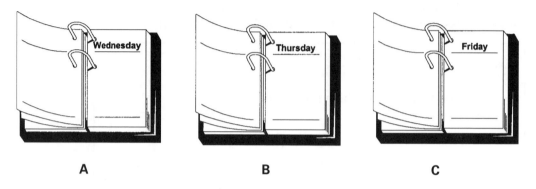

   A   **B**   **C**

5 Who will arrive late at the meeting?

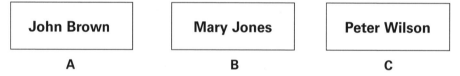

John Brown	Mary Jones	Peter Wilson
A	**B**	**C**

6 What does the annual report show about sales of clothes?

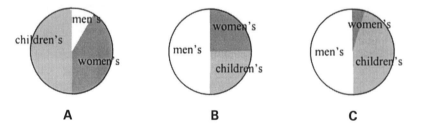

   A   **B**   **C**

7 Which flight is the man going to take to Paris?

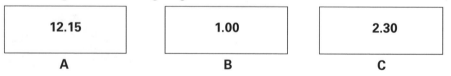

12.15	1.00	2.30
A	**B**	**C**

8 Which is the cheapest model?

   A Romex
   B Wilton
   C Asset

PART TWO

Questions 9–15

- Look at the notes below.
- Some information is missing.
- You will hear an interview between Anna Marsh, who works for a business magazine, and Jim Davenport, who works in the publicity department of a company, Gold Express.
- For each question **9–15**, fill in the missing information in the numbered space using a **word**, **numbers**, or **letters**.
- After you have listened once, replay the recording.

Interview notes

Company: GOLD EXPRESS

Started in: **(9)**   ....

Most recent turnover: **(10)**   ....

Growth over 5 years: **(11)**   .... %.

Managing Director: Peter   **(12)**   ....

Total number of customers: **(13)**   ....

Number of employees: **(14)**   ....

Recent staff questionnaire showed: **(15)**   .... % enjoyed their work.

PART THREE

Questions 16–22

- Look at the notes below.
- Some information is missing.
- You will hear part of a business news programme.
- For each question **16–22**, fill in the missing information in the numbered space using **one** or **two** words.
- After you have listened once, replay the recording.

Waymans

Company to sell	**(16)**	.... business.
Reason for sale:	**(17)**	....
Company changes began in	**(18)**	....
Money from sale likely to fund	**(19)**	....

Teltalk

David Driver to be new	**(20)**	....
Teltalk to merge with a	**(21)**	.... company.
11% share will be bought by	**(22)**	.... firm.

PART FOUR

Questions 23–30

- You will hear an interview with a woman who publishes magazines.
- For each question **23–30**, mark one letter (**A**, **B** or **C**) for the correct answer.
- After you have listened once, replay the recording.

23 Sally wanted to borrow one billion pounds to

    A   start a new company.
    B   purchase a large company.
    C   expand a small company.

24 Sally got the money for her company, *Close Communications*, from

    A   a bank.
    B   social contacts.
    C   her business partner.

25 Sally recruited her staff by

    A   inviting candidates for a meal.
    B   contacting former colleagues.
    C   advertising in newspapers.

26 *Close Communications* encourages its employees to travel by

    A   car.
    B   train.
    C   bicycle.

27 If *Close Communications* is successful, the staff will receive

    A   a bonus payment.
    B   a pay rise.
    C   a share in the profits.

28 For their offices, all staff were given

    A   a budget to spend on furniture.
    B   the same kind of furniture.
    C   a limited choice of furniture.

29 Sally thinks that people are usually unhappy at work because

    A   their salaries are too low.

    B   there are too many forms to complete.

    C   there is too much management control.

30 In their first year, *Close Communications* will produce

    A   2 magazines.

    B   9 magazines.

    C   16 magazines.

You now have 10 minutes to transfer your answers to your Answer Sheet.

SPEAKING   12 minutes

PART 1

The interview – about 2 minutes

In this part the interlocutor asks questions to each of the candidates in turn. You have to give information about yourself and express personal opinions.

PART 2

'Mini presentation' – about 5 minutes

In this part of the test you are asked to give a short talk on a business topic. You have to choose one of the topics from the two below and then talk for about one minute. You have one minute to prepare your ideas.

A   WHAT IS IMPORTANT WHEN . . .?

CHOOSING A HOTEL FOR BUSINESS VISITORS

- **LOCATION**
- **COST**
- **STANDARD**

B   WHAT IS IMPORTANT WHEN . . .?

EMPLOYING A SECRETARY

- **EXPERIENCE**
- **SKILLS**
- **PERSONAL QUALITIES**

PART 3

Discussion – about 5 minutes

In this part of the test the examiner reads out a scenario and gives you some prompt material in the form of pictures or words. You have 30 seconds to look at the prompt card, an example of which is below, and then about 2 minutes to discuss the scenario with your partner. After that the examiner will ask you more questions related to the topic.

For **two** or **three** candidates

Scenario

I'm going to describe a situation.

A company is sending one of its staff on his first business trip to another country. Talk together for about 2 minutes about the different things he needs to take and decide which 3 things would be most useful.

Here are some ideas to help you.

Prompt material

Test 3

READING AND WRITING   1 hour 30 minutes

READING

PART ONE

Questions 1–5

- Look at the questions **1–5**.
- In each question, which sentence is correct?
- For each question, mark one letter (**A**, **B**, or **C**) on your Answer Sheet.

Example: 0

> Don't forget -
>
> flight BA692   6.45 pm

The plane arrives at

A   quarter to seven in the morning.
B   quarter past six in the evening.
C   quarter to seven in the evening.

The correct answer is **C**, so mark your Answer Sheet like this:

0	A	B	C
	▯	▯	▬

1

> 26/6 – 11 am URGENT MESSAGE FOR JENNIFER RUSSELL.
> YOUR FLIGHT TO ISTANBUL TOMORROW IS NOW POSTPONED TO
> 06.15 – 28/6.

When will Mrs Russell fly to Istanbul?

A   26 June
B   27 June
C   28 June

2

> *When collecting parcels from this post office, you will need to produce documentation which proves your identity.*

    A   You cannot post parcels from here without documentation.
    B   You should collect post and documents at the same time.
    C   You must bring something in writing showing who you are.

3

> **If you do not wish to be sent product information leaflets**
>
> **please tick this box** ☐

    A   Leave the box empty if you don't mind receiving information.
    B   Fill in the box if you need more information.
    C   Tick the box if you are happy with our products.

4

> **Mayfield College**
> **Italian for Business**
>
> 5×3-hour lessons
> twice weekly
> beginning Tuesday 28 September

Each lesson will last

    A   2 hours.
    B   3 hours.
    C   5 hours.

5

> **MANUFACTURER'S NOTICE**
> Please return any goods damaged during transportation
> within two weeks of delivery, for immediate replacement.

    A   Goods damaged during transportation must be replaced immediately.
    B   If this product arrives damaged, send it back within a fortnight.
    C   If you require a refund, send the product back immediately.

PART TWO

Questions 6–10

- Look at the list of job vacancies below.
- For questions **6–10**, decide which vacancy (**A–H**) is the most suitable for each person at the bottom of the page.
- For each question, mark the correct letter (**A–H**) on your Answer Sheet.
- Do not use any letter more than once.

Bretlands Employment Agency

Bretlands have the following vacancies for staff

A	Director of Finance
B	Director of Quality Control
C	Sales Manager
D	Transport Manager
E	Assistant Personnel Manager
F	Designer in Publicity Department
G	Technician in IT Department
H	Assistant in Legal Department

---

6   Tom has a lot of experience preparing the layout for brochures on computer.

7   Christine recently got a qualification in computer programming.

8   Peter has worked as an accountant in a large company for twelve years.

9   Mark has passed a law exam at school and would like to use this knowledge in his job.

10   Jane works in a human resources department, helping to recruit staff.

PART THREE

Questions 11–15

- Look at the graphs below. They show the number of vehicles sold compared with the number leased by eight different retailers during the year 2000.
- Which chart does each sentence (**11–15**) on the opposite page describe?
- For each sentence, mark one letter (**A–H**) on your Answer Sheet.
- Do not use any letter more than once.

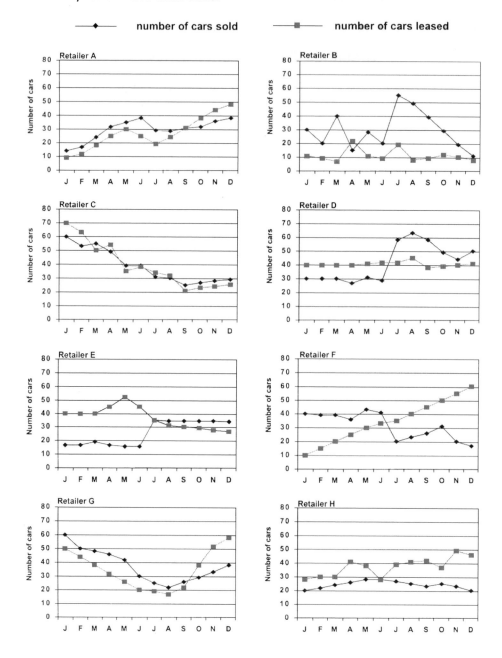

11 Leases grew more rapidly than sales in the second half of the year, following a steady rise in both sectors earlier in the year.

12 Vehicle sales rose sharply in the middle of the year, overtaking leases which nevertheless rose slightly in the last quarter.

13 While the vehicle lease business expanded during the year, vehicle sales dipped sharply after six months, never recovering their early high level.

14 The number of vehicles leased remained low throughout the year, rising only briefly above sales, which fluctuated dramatically in the first six months.

15 After falling steadily for much of the year, both sales and leases recovered, with the number of leases eventually exceeding sales.

PART FOUR

Questions 16–22

- Read the magazine article below about a jewellery designer.
- Are sentences **16–22** on the opposite page 'Right' or 'Wrong'? If there is not enough information to answer 'Right' or 'Wrong', choose 'Doesn't say'.
- For each sentence **16–22**, mark one letter (**A**, **B** or **C**) on your Answer Sheet.

The jewellery designer

He was young and completely unknown, but Paul Waterhouse believed in himself. He'd heard that there was going to be a large exhibition for jewellery designers and he asked the organisers whether he could show some of his work. 'I was only 21,' he says, 'and they agreed, if I could show a complete collection.' So he went to the bank, borrowed £1,500 for materials, and began to work on new designs. 'The exhibition was fantastic. Although everyone else was much more experienced than I was, my designs were still praised.'

He decided to transfer his business to Canada and began to experiment with new materials: all sorts of stones from around the world, some totally new to him. 'As most of them weren't precious, it changed the way I approached design. It was great! I was able to produce much larger pieces of modern jewellery,' he says. 'Then I was asked by an advertising agency to design a wedding ring for a TV advert. The agency liked what I'd done, but their client, a car manufacturer, wanted something a little more traditional. I was happy to make changes and that work gave me a lot of free publicity.'

16 At the start of his career, Paul felt confident.

    A Right   **B** Wrong   **C** Doesn't say

17 Paul used his savings to make jewellery for the exhibition.

    A Right   **B** Wrong   **C** Doesn't say

18 People at the exhibition admired his designs.

    A Right   **B** Wrong   **C** Doesn't say

19 Paul's first shop opened in Canada.

    A Right   **B** Wrong   **C** Doesn't say

20 Paul prefers working with valuable materials.

    A Right   **B** Wrong   **C** Doesn't say

21 Paul uses an advertising agency to promote his jewellery.

    A Right   **B** Wrong   **C** Doesn't say

22 Paul was willing to compromise on the design of the ring.

    A Right   **B** Wrong   **C** Doesn't say

PART FIVE

Questions 23–28

- Read the article below about computer software.
- For each question **23–28**, on the opposite page, choose the correct answer.
- Mark one letter (**A**, **B** or **C**) on your Answer Sheet.

Computer software

As more and more companies are using the Internet to do business, Mark Williams explains how a new software package is helping the efficient transfer of medicines from factory to patient.

AHL Pharmaceuticals is one of Britain's largest wholesale distributors of medicines. Under a European parent company, Setra AG, it covers 40 per cent of the British market. The company buys medicines from the manufacturers and delivers them on a twice-daily basis to hundreds of hospitals and pharmacies around the country.

'The responsibility for supplying such large quantities of medicines is frightening,' says IT director, Stephen Smith. 'If a manufacturer has quality control problems, creating a shortfall in supply, or if medicines are suddenly needed in large quantities somewhere else in the world our stock levels can fall dramatically. In the past such a lack of balance between supply and demand was a huge problem. With our new software system, we know immediately of any possible manufacturing or supply difficulties, can warn our customers and suggest possible alternatives.'

This system is so efficient because manufacturers can update details themselves of stock levels and product information. Twice a day staff at AHL transfer this data to their main computer system where it is made available through the AHL website to company personnel and customers.

With so many people having access to the data, isn't the security of the system at risk? 'Not at all,' says Smith. 'We run the software within our own internal security system. The data goes into a special "sandbox" which is separate from the rest of the system. Even if someone manages to get into the software, they can't go anywhere else on the network.'

And does he think that this is the limit of the software's use? 'The first time I saw this I had the feeling that life would be different from now on. Instead of having lots of pieces of paper flying around, an expansion of the software system into the purchasing department means that orders can now be dealt with in a moment. The only delay to further expansion is deciding what area of the company to apply it to next.'

23 AHL Pharmaceuticals

    A   manufactures medicines.

    B   puts drug companies in contact with customers.

    C   supplies medicines to customers.

24 According to the text, what is the challenge for pharmaceutical manufacturers?

    A   developing new types of medicines

    B   transporting medicines to other countries

    C   ensuring a constant supply of medicines

25 The most important function of the new software is to

    A   maintain the quality of customer service.

    B   expand the customer network worldwide.

    C   inform patients about better quality medicines.

26 New information about medicines

    A   is updated by the manufacturers twice a day.

    B   is made available to customers by AHL personnel.

    C   is given direct to customers by manufacturers.

27 Stephen Smith feels that

    A   the security of information on the network used to be a worry.

    B   all the data should be stored on the same system.

    C   the company's computer-based information is well-protected.

28 The new software

    A   can be used in many areas of the company's business.

    B   will soon totally replace the need for paper documents.

    C   is delaying the expansion of the purchasing department.

PART SIX

Questions 29–40

- Read the newspaper article below about the creation of new jobs.
- Choose the correct word to fill each gap, from **A**, **B** or **C** on the opposite page.
- For each question **29–40**, mark one letter (**A**, **B** or **C**) on your Answer Sheet.

NEW JOBS

A new clothing company is hoping to create as (**29**) .... as 500 jobs in its factory and nationwide chain of stores. The company, *New Trend* was set (**30**) .... by Peter Dalton, a 36-year-old businessman (**31**) .... Liverpool.

The company, (**32**) .... is due to start production early next year, will provide employment (**33**) .... 300 people in its factory on the edge of Liverpool. In 12 months' time, (**34**) .... will be a further 200 jobs, as the company begins opening shops in towns in (**35**) .... parts of Britain.

Peter Dalton is also (**36**) .... to open a shop in New York. He hopes that (**37**) .... this shop proves successful, the chain (**38**) .... expand across the whole of North America.

'This project has (**39**) .... me over four years to finalise,' says Peter Dalton, 'and (**40**) .... that it's finally getting started, I'm really excited.'

---

29 **A** much   **B** many   **C** lot

30 **A** to   **B** in   **C** up

31 **A** from   **B** at   **C** of

32 **A** who   **B** which   **C** what

33 **A** by   **B** on   **C** for

34 **A** it   **B** they   **C** there

35 **A** any   **B** all   **C** every

36 **A** plans   **B** planning   **C** planner

37 **A** if   **B** unless   **C** whether

38 **A** could   **B** ought   **C** needs

39 **A** took   **B** taken   **C** taking

40 **A** so   **B** when   **C** now

PART SEVEN

Questions 41–45

- Read the memo and advertisement below.
- Complete the form at the bottom of the page.
- Write a word or phrase (in CAPITAL LETTERS) or a number on lines **41–45** on your Answer Sheet.

Northern Software

24 Queens Road, Chapeltown

To: Jean Palmer, Purchasing
From: Tom Milton, Accounts
Date: 1 March 2002
Subject: Envelopes

We've run out of the envelopes we use for mailing invoices – the white ones with windows. I need some more tomorrow – I don't want to delay sending the customer bills this month, so please order the envelopes today, and have them delivered as soon as possible. I've got about 200 invoices to post.

HAYES OFFICE SUPPLIES

Reductions on some product lines

Brown or white envelopes (supplied in quantities of 100, 500 or 1000)
– 15% off catalogue price

Product code: EV300 (plain) or EV311 (with window)

Three delivery services available:
one week (free)
four days (minimum charge £2)
next day (minimum charge £5)
101 Leeds Road, Chapeltown
Tel: 275 9087 Fax: 275 9088

ORDER FORM

Company name: **(41)** ....

Delivery address: **(42)** ...., *Chapeltown*

Product code: **(43)** ....

Colour: **(44)** ....

Quantity: *500*

Delivery service required: **(45)** ....

WRITING

PART ONE

Question 46

- You work for an international company in Los Angeles.
- You have arranged to meet a colleague, Carole Buckley, in the New York office on 3 February.
- Write an **email** to your colleague:
  - confirming the date of your visit to New York
  - suggesting what time the meeting should start
  - inviting her to dinner after the meeting.

- Write about **30–40** words on your Answer Sheet.

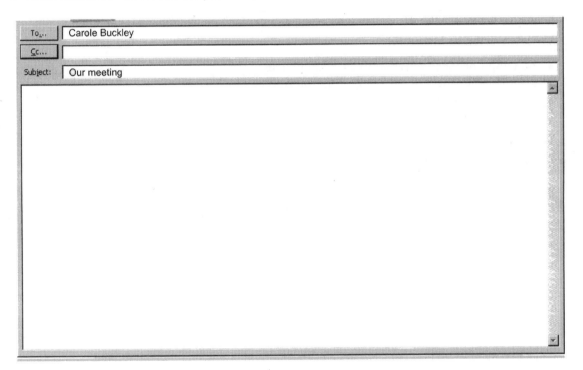

PART TWO

Question 47

● Read this note you have received from your boss.

Mary Brown at Head Office called to invite staff from our branch to have a tour round their new building. Could you reply? 20 people definitely want to go.

She wants to know which departments we'd be most interested in seeing. She didn't say anything about what time the tour would start. Could you please check?

Thanks.

● Write an **email** to Ms Brown:

- ● thanking her for the invitation to Head Office
- ● telling her how many people are planning to go
- ● saying which departments people would like to see
- ● asking about the time of the visit.

● Write **60–80** words on your Answer Sheet.
● Do not include postal addresses.

LISTENING   Approximately 40 minutes (including 10 minutes' transfer time)

PART ONE

Questions 1–8

- For questions **1–8** you will hear eight short recordings.
- For each question, mark one letter (**A**, **B**, or **C**) for the correct answer.

Example:

When were the machine parts sent?

Monday 31st	Tuesday 1st	Thursday 3rd
A	**B**	**C**

The answer is A.

After you have listened once, replay each recording.

1   Where is the Emerald Airlines office?

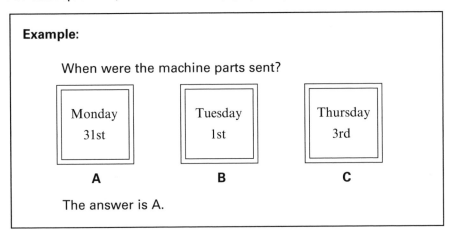

2   When will they deliver the new computer?

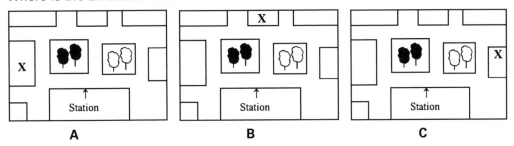

3   Which chart shows foreign trade this year?

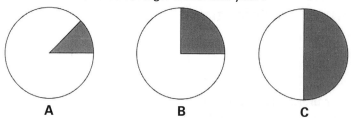

A   B   C

4   Which product does the man still need?

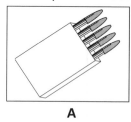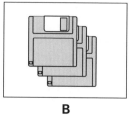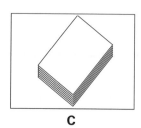

A   B   C

5   What is Helen's degree in?

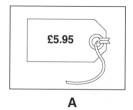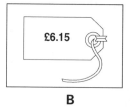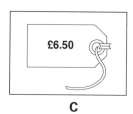

| computing | languages | management |
| A | B | C |

6   How much per metre will the woman pay?

£5.95   £6.15   £6.50

A   B   C

7   Who are the speakers?

| a manager and his assistant | colleagues from the same department | a businessman and a customer |
| A | B | C |

8   Which chart is correct?

A   B   C

PART TWO

Questions 9–15

- Look at the notes below.
- Some information is missing.
- You will hear a woman booking a train ticket.
- For each question **9–15**, fill in the missing information in the numbered space using a **word**, **numbers**, or **letters**.
- After you have listened once, replay the recording.

Sales trip to Paris – train details

Departure time: **(9)** ....

Train number: **(10)** ....

Coach and seat number: **(11)** ....

Price charged: **(12)** ....

Check-in desk: **(13)** ....

Booking reference: **(14)** ....

Contact name: **(15)** ....

PART THREE

Questions 16–22

- Look at the notes below.
- Some information is missing.
- You will hear Alan French, the Managing Director of A2Z Racing, talking at a public meeting about his future plans.
- For each question **16–22**, fill in the missing information in the numbered space using **one** or **two** words.
- After you have listened once, replay the recording.

NEW RACETRACK IN BRAMFORD

New racetrack will be where the **(16)** .... used to be.

Work begins: **(17)** ....

PARTNERS: SPC and Runwells

SPC will provide an on-site **(18)** .... and a sports café.

Runwells manufacture **(19)** ....

Runwells will provide everyone with **(20)** ....

TRACK USE:

– racing twice a month
– Police and ambulance need it for **(21)** .... their drivers.

FUTURE PLANS:

– possibility of building a **(22)** ....

PART FOUR

Questions 23–30

- You will hear a discussion between a radio interviewer and the owners of two companies which sell sandwiches.
- For each question **23–30**, mark one letter (**A**, **B** or **C**) for the correct answer.
- After you have listened once, replay the recording.

23 What problem did Brian have with his sandwich business?

   A   His first shop was unpopular.
   B   He had to close one of the shops.
   C   His second shop didn't open on time.

24 Brian says his success is due to

   A   quick service.
   B   quality food.
   C   cheap prices.

25 Brian says the trend nowadays is for his customers to

   A   buy a sandwich to eat at their desk.
   B   smoke in the street at lunchtime.
   C   take a couple of breaks in the day.

26 Brian says the average British lunch break is

   A   just over 30 minutes.
   B   more than 45 minutes.
   C   about 60 minutes.

27 Geraldine started her sandwich business because she

   A   had always wanted to work with food.
   B   recognised a good business opportunity.
   C   was unsuccessful as a journalist.

28 At the beginning, Geraldine financed her business

   A   through her parents.
   B   with a bank loan.
   C   with her own money.

29 After Geraldine found premises, it was difficult for her to

A run both parts of the business.
B find enough clients to deliver to.
C afford the rent of the building.

30 When Jack first agreed to help Geraldine, he was

A in debt.
B on holiday.
C out of work.

> **You now have 10 minutes to transfer your answers to your Answer Sheet.**

SPEAKING   12 minutes

SAMPLE SPEAKING TASKS

PART 1

The interview – about 2 minutes

In this part the interlocutor asks questions to each of the candidates in turn. You have to give information about yourself and express personal opinions.

PART 2

'Mini presentation' – about 5 minutes

In this part of the test you are asked to give a short talk on a business topic. You have to choose one of the topics from the two below and then talk for about one minute. You have one minute to prepare your ideas.

A   WHAT IS IMPORTANT WHEN . . .?

GOING FOR A JOB INTERVIEW

- **KNOWLEDGE OF COMPANY**
- **APPEARANCE**
- **ARRIVING ON TIME**

B   WHAT IS IMPORTANT WHEN . . .?

MAKING TRAVEL ARRANGEMENTS FOR A BUSINESS TRIP

- **CONVENIENCE**
- **COST**
- **COMFORT**

PART 3

Discussion – about 5 minutes

In this part of the test the examiner reads out a scenario and gives you some prompt material in the form of pictures or words. You have 30 seconds to look at the prompt card, an example of which is below, and then about 2 minutes to discuss the scenario with your partner. After that the examiner will ask you more questions related to the topic.

For **two** or **three** candidates

Scenario

I'm going to describe a situation.

A company is planning to introduce a general training programme for new staff. Talk together about the topics the company could include in the programme and decide which 3 you think are most important.

Here are some ideas to help you.

Prompt material

GENERAL TRAINING PROGRAMME FOR NEW STAFF

Topics for training

- Equipment
- Computer skills
- Company organisation
- Company rules
- Customer service
- Product training
- Health and safety
- Foreign languages

Test 4

READING AND WRITING   1 hour 30 minutes

READING

PART ONE

Questions 1–5

- Look at the questions **1–5**.
- In each question, which sentence is correct?
- For each question, mark one letter (**A**, **B**, or **C**) on your Answer Sheet.

Example: 0

Don't forget -

flight BA692   6.45 pm

The plane arrives at

A   quarter to seven in the morning.
B   quarter past six in the evening.
C   quarter to seven in the evening.

The correct answer is **C**, so mark your Answer Sheet like this:

0	A	B	C
	☐	☐	▬

1

John, I haven't had a chance to phone Bill. Have you? Liz

A   Liz has tried unsuccessfully to phone Bill.
B   Liz is asking John to phone Bill.
C   Liz has been too busy to phone Bill.

2

> **Order any stationery from this catalogue in June and receive a**
> **special free pen.**

A   Ask for our June catalogue and get some free stationery.
B   Buy a product in June and you'll get a gift.
C   Order a pen before June and get another one free.

3

> We expect all debts to be settled within seven days. Please note credit
> cards are not accepted.

You can pay

A   by credit card within seven days.
B   in weekly instalments.
C   by cheque or cash within one week.

4

> *NOTICE FOR HOTEL GUESTS*
>
> **When car park is locked (midnight – 6 am), contact security guard**
> **for entry.**

A   The hotel offers safe parking for guests' cars at night.
B   Guests can only leave their cars here during the day.
C   There is no entry to this car park after midnight.

5

> **Coffee is served during the morning break to delegates**
> **attending the product demonstration**

A   Coffee will be available during the meeting if requested.
B   There is a coffee break for participants during the morning.
C   Delegates can see a product demonstration while they have coffee.

PART TWO

Questions 6–10

- Look at the list below. It shows the titles of office files in a manufacturing company.
- For questions **6–10**, decide which file (**A–H**) each person at the bottom of the page should look at.
- For each question, mark one letter (**A–H**) on your Answer Sheet.
- Do not use any letter more than once.

Office Files

A	Sales figures
B	Customer contact information
C	Complaints about faulty goods
D	Product details
E	Publicity expenditure
F	Service agreements
G	Shipping
H	Human Resources

---

6 Ms Kay has to find some missing documentation for an export order.

7 Mr Brooks wants to check some costs for the advertising campaign he is planning.

8 Mr Tanner needs to know the exact measurements of the new desks he is selling.

9 Ms Grafton needs the email address of a regular client.

10 Mrs Anders wants to compare how well two successful products are performing.

PART THREE

Questions 11–15

- Look at the charts below. They show the expenditure on advertising compared to the increase in sales income of 8 companies over a 3-year period.
- Which chart does each sentence (**11–15**) on the opposite page describe?
- For each sentence, mark one letter (**A–H**) on your Answer Sheet.
- Do not use any letter more than once.

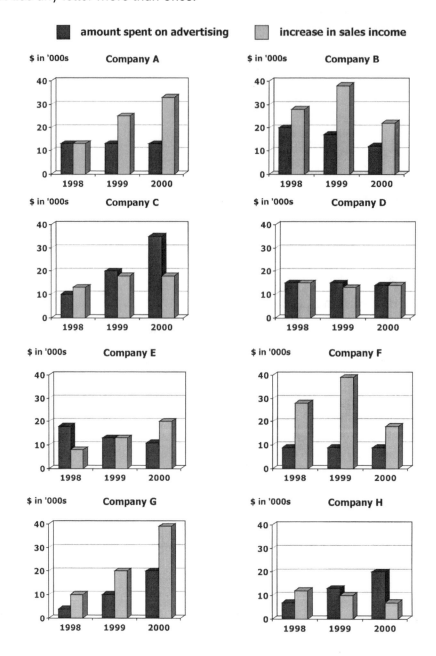

11   The company benefited from a steady rise in income across the period in spite of an annual decrease in expenditure on advertising.

12   The annual increases in spending on advertising had no positive effect on income which continued to fall over the period.

13   Although advertising spending remained unchanged during the 3 years, increase in income fluctuated, reaching a peak in the middle of the period.

14   Both advertising costs and income from sales rose over the whole period, with sales at about double the level of advertising spending in 2000.

15   Even though the amount of money spent on advertising went up year on year, the increase in income levelled off in 2000.

PART FOUR

Questions 16–22

- Read the advertisement below about health insurance.
- Are sentences **16–22** on the opposite page 'Right' or 'Wrong'? If there is not enough information to answer 'Right' or 'Wrong', choose 'Doesn't say'.
- For each sentence **16–22**, mark one letter (**A**, **B** or **C**) on your Answer Sheet.

HEALTHSURE – for you and your family

Many health insurance policies only cover the payments you have to make when you go into hospital, but with *Healthsure*, you are refunded for routine visits as well. In addition, we guarantee to refund you within 2 to 4 weeks.

Healthsure is an organisation which puts the interests of its members before profits. This means we offer very low membership rates. On average, £1.40 is debited from your bank account each week, so you won't ever need to worry about forgetting to send payment.

It's easy to join *Healthsure*. Just fill in the application form and name the members of your family you wish to include on the policy. If you, your partner, or one of your children has to go into hospital, we will pay a daily allowance. These cash payments are not taxed, and we aim to deal with claims within 72 hours. So, why wait any longer? Apply now and benefit from our caring approach to health care.

Phone us free on 0800 885511 (24-hour number) for further information from our customer service advisers.

---

16 *Healthsure* makes direct payments to hospitals for its customers.

    A Right   **B** Wrong   **C** Doesn't say

17 *Healthsure* makes an annual profit.

    A Right   **B** Wrong   **C** Doesn't say

18 Customers must pay *Healthsure* monthly instalments.

    A Right   **B** Wrong   **C** Doesn't say

19 *Healthsure* will insure children and their parents on the same policy.

    A Right   **B** Wrong   **C** Doesn't say

20 Tax is payable on the daily allowances customers receive.

    A Right   **B** Wrong   **C** Doesn't say

21 Membership applications are approved in less than 72 hours.

    A Right   **B** Wrong   **C** Doesn't say

22 You can contact *Healthsure* at any time.

    A Right   **B** Wrong   **C** Doesn't say

PART FIVE

Questions 23–28

- Read the article below about a chain of restaurants.
- For each question **23–28**, on the opposite page, choose the correct answer.
- Mark one letter (**A**, **B** or **C**) on your Answer Sheet.

A GROWING RESTAURANT CHAIN

Simon Dale, the chairman and founder of the Dalehouse restaurant chain, yesterday announced plans to open a further 20 restaurants and create 600 new jobs in the next four years. The group hopes to open 4 of the new restaurants by the end of this year, creating up to 120 jobs. The programme will result in a chain of over 100 Dalehouse restaurants in towns and cities all over the United Kingdom by the end of the four-year period.

The company also has a limited programme of expansion in other countries. There are plans for the company to open its third restaurant abroad towards the middle of next year as planning permission was recently received for a restaurant in the south of Spain. At the moment there is a Dalehouse restaurant in Germany and another in Denmark. Negotiations are already taking place about opening two more restaurants in Germany and three more in Spain.

Mr Dale said yesterday: 'Our plans are ambitious and there is no doubt that in some ways they are quite frightening. But we've been in business for twenty years and a lot of our staff have been with us for most of that time and, as a result, have experience of things growing at a fast rate.'

The Dalehouse chain currently has 82 restaurants, all in town centre locations. The group is planning now to expand further in residential areas. The company intends to continue its tradition of having most of its restaurants open from midday until midnight seven days a week. It will also continue to open restaurants in buildings which were originally designed for a different purpose.

Certain financial journalists wonder whether the company will be able to find enough cash to finance its plans. Mr Dale, however, remains positive. 'It is true,' he says, 'that we will not be able to finance the plans without some support from the banks, and we are in the process of arranging this at the moment. Most of the money, however, will come from the amount we have kept back from our profits for future investment in the business. We opened 4 restaurants last year so an expansion programme of 5 this year and 6 next would not be outside the normal rate of growth. We have had hardly any problems financing our expansion in the past and expect this to continue in the future.

23 After four years there will be

A a total of 600 people employed by Dalehouse restaurants.

B a Dalehouse restaurant in over 120 UK towns and cities.

C 20 more Dalehouse restaurants than there are at present.

24 How many Dalehouse restaurants are there in other countries at the moment?

A One.

B Two.

C Three.

25 What does Mr Dale say about the company's employees?

A Most of them have worked for Dalehouse since it started.

B Most of them have enjoyed being in a growing company.

C Many of them have seen the company develop quickly.

26 What will be different about the new Dalehouse restaurants?

A Some will be away from town centres.

B Some will be in buildings not planned as restaurants.

C Some will be open every day of the week.

27 What does Mr Dale have to say about financing the company's plans?

A Dalehouse has already arranged loans to help with the finance.

B Dalehouse will need help from the banks.

C Dalehouse has enough money to finance its plans without help.

28 What does Mr Dale say about problems caused by expansion?

A There have only been minor problems.

B There will be fewer problems in the future.

C There have been very few problems.

PART SIX

Questions 29–40

- Read the article below about time management.
- Choose the correct word to fill each gap, from **A**, **B** or **C** on the opposite page.
- For each question **29–40**, mark **one** letter (**A**, **B** or **C**) on your Answer Sheet.

Time management

Until recently, books on how to manage your time at work were seen as a bit of a joke in the business world. Many were enjoyable to read (**29**) .... weren't taken seriously. (**30**) .... told their readers to dress well, be positive, decide (**31**) .... they were going and then use (**32**) .... valuable minute to make sure they got there. One very successful book, first published twenty years (**33**) .... and still available in bookshops, is The One-Minute Manager. It tells the story of a keen young man who wants to learn (**34**) .... about how to be a top-performing executive. The authors believe that most people (**35**) .... the day putting (**36**) .... problems, or when they do try to solve (**37**) ...., don't do enough. According (**38**) .... the authors, having achievable targets should be a manager's aim. Managers everywhere should read (**39**) .... book carefully, in order to benefit from (**40**) .... sensible advice.

---

29 **A** but   **B** or   **C** even

30 **A** It   **B** They   **C** We

31 **A** where   **B** who   **C** why

32 **A** some   **B** all   **C** every

33 **A** before   **B** ago   **C** since

34 **A** lot   **B** much   **C** more

35 **A** spend   **B** spending **C** spent

36 **A** about   **B** over   **C** off

37 **A** them   **B** these   **C** those

38 **A** for   **B** from   **C** to

39 **A** the   **B** one   **C** a

40 **A** their   **B** his   **C** its

PART SEVEN

Questions 41–45

- Read the note and the leaflet below.
- Complete the invoice at the bottom of the page.
- Write a word or phrase (in CAPITAL LETTERS) or a number on lines **41–45** on your Answer Sheet.

Marta

Can you send Star Employment an invoice for their latest advertisement. It was for a half page ad in Recruitment Today. I don't think it was colour. Can you state on the invoice they need to pay within 7 days, not the usual 14 days. It needs to go to Mr Gordon.

Thanks

Jean-Pierre

Southern Newspaper Group
- titles include
the Daily Record
Business Network magazine and
Recruitment Today

Advertising Rates:

	Black/white	Colour
Full page	£250	£425
Half page	£150	£255
Quarter page	£90	£155

Deadline for advertisements: Thursdays 5.30pm

INVOICE TO:

Company	**(41)** ....
	150 – 162 Browning Street
	Castleford
For the attention of:	**(42)** ....
Publication:	**(43)** ....
Size of advertisement:	**(44)** ....
Cost:	**(45)** ....
Payment Terms:	7 days

WRITING

PART ONE

Question 46

- You are attending a conference in the USA next week and will need secretarial help during the trip as your PA is away on holiday.
- Write a **memo** to the Human Resources Manager:

  - requesting a temporary PA for the trip
  - explaining why your PA cannot go with you
  - giving the dates of the trip.

- Write about **30–40** words on your Answer Sheet.

MEMO

To: ....

From: ....

Date: 11 March 2002

Subject: Temporary PA

PART TWO

Question 47

● Read this part of a fax from Sally Saunders, a hotel conference manager.

To: ....

Fax No: ....

From: Sally Saunders

Date: 1 March 2002

Pages (incl cover):   3

Thank you very much for your letter, enquiring about availability of conference facilities at this hotel for 1–4 September. I note your request for a special menu for the conference dinner on your final evening. You will find suggestions enclosed.

Unfortunately, during the week you have chosen for your conference, there is a trade fair. Therefore, we have very few single rooms available. I could offer you twin-bedded rooms, or perhaps you would consider moving your conference to the following week?

I look forward to receiving your booking and choice of dishes for the conference dinner.

● Write a **fax** to Mrs Saunders:

- thanking her for her fax
- confirming your original dates for the conference
- booking 20 twin-bedded rooms
- telling her which dishes from the menu you require for the conference dinner.

● Write **60–80** words on your Answer Sheet.
● Do not include postal addresses.

LISTENING   Approximately 40 minutes (including 10 minutes transfer time)

PART ONE

Questions 1–8

- For questions **1–8** you will hear eight short recordings.
- For each question, mark one letter (**A**, **B**, or **C**) for the correct answer.

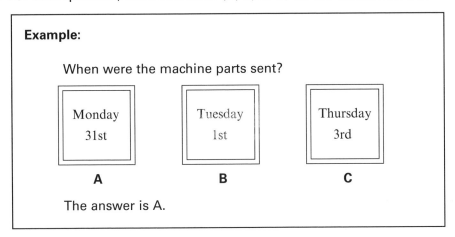

Example:

When were the machine parts sent?

Monday 31st	Tuesday 1st	Thursday 3rd
A	**B**	**C**

The answer is A.

After you have listened once, replay each recording.

1   Which department has a vacancy at the moment?

A   Personnel
B   Sales
C   Production

2   How will Dover Tools dispatch the order?

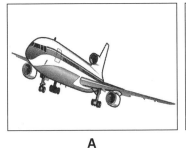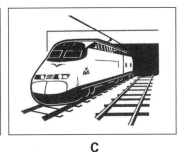

A	B	C

3   What is the message for Mr Brown?

Jane Kelly will ring again.	Please phone Jane Kelly back.	Jane Kelly called to see you.
A	**B**	**C**

97

4   When will production start?

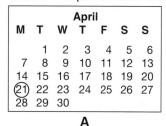 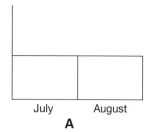 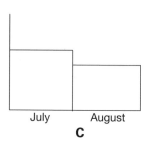

A   **B**   **C**

5   Which chart are the two women talking about?

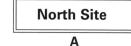 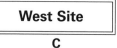

A   **B**   **C**

6   Which car park will close during repair work?

North Site   **East Site**   **West Site**

A   **B**   **C**

7   When are the two people going to meet?

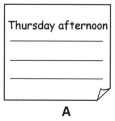  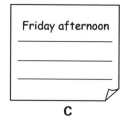

Thursday afternoon   Friday morning   Friday afternoon

A   **B**   **C**

8   Which graph is correct?

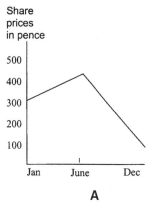  

A   **B**   **C**

PART TWO

Questions 9–15

- Look at the notes below.
- Some information is missing.
- You will hear a man contacting an employment agency about the recruitment of temporary staff for his business.
- For each question **9–15**, fill in the missing information in the numbered space using a **word**, **numbers**, or **letters**.
- After you have listened once, replay the recording.

Advance Recruitment

Company name: A & T Computer Solutions

Contact name: **(9)**   John ....

Number of staff needed: **(10)** ....

Starting date: **(11)** .... October 2000

Length of contract: minimum of   **(12)** .... weeks

Number of hours: 40 per week

Rate quoted: **(13)** £ .... per hour

Contact telephone number: **(14)** .... extension 218

Location of A & T Computer
Solutions: **(15)** .... Business Park on Broad Street

---

PART THREE

Questions 16–22

- Look at the notes below.
- Some information is missing.
- You will hear a management consultant giving a business studies lecture about MTF, a company that manufactures heating systems.
- For each question **16–22**, fill in the missing information in the numbered space using **one** or **two** words.
- After you have listened once, replay the recording.

MTF Ltd.
Heating Systems Manufacturer

Date company started   (**16**) ....

Company's market position due to   (**17**) ....

Plans to invest in   (**18**) ....

Rewards employees with   (**19**) ....

Training programme has received   (**20**) .... (from local government)

Promotes staff with good   (**21**) ....

Business section needing improvement: (**22**) ....

PART FOUR

Questions 23–30

- You will hear a radio interview with a representative of the New Zealand Kiwi Fruit Marketing Board (the KMB), about the sale and export of kiwi fruit.
- For each question **23–30**, mark one letter (**A**, **B** or **C**) for the correct answer.
- After you have listened once, replay the recording.

23 New Zealand's highest earning exports are

   A   dairy products.
   B   fruit and vegetables.
   C   lamb and wool.

24 Peter Bull says that the KMB was set up in order to increase

   A   the profits of retailers.
   B   the number of growers.
   C   the demand for kiwi fruit.

25 In order to sell kiwi fruit abroad, the KMB relies on

   A   low prices.
   B   quality control.
   C   TV advertising.

26 The newest export markets are

   A   the Middle East and Korea.
   B   Europe and Japan.
   C   South America and Vietnam.

27 What percentage of New Zealand's total exports are kiwi fruit?

   A   seven
   B   twenty-five
   C   thirty-two

28 Kiwi fruit are transported from farms to ports by

   A   air.
   B   rail.
   C   road.

29 How does the KMB want to improve the shipping of kiwi fruit?

    A   by increasing the number of ships it uses

    B   by improving the way the fruit is packed

    C   by lowering the temperature on the ships

30 What is the most popular type of fruit in New Zealand?

    A   apples

    B   kiwi fruit

    C   pears

You now have 10 minutes to transfer your answers to your Answer Sheet.

SPEAKING   12 minutes

SAMPLE SPEAKING TASKS

PART 1

The interview – about 2 minutes

In this part the interlocutor asks questions to each of the candidates in turn. You have to give information about yourself and express personal opinions.

PART 2

'Mini presentation' – about 5 minutes

In this part of the test you are asked to give a short talk on a business topic. You have to choose one of the topics from the two below and then talk for about one minute. You have one minute to prepare your ideas.

A   WHAT IS IMPORTANT WHEN . . .?

ORGANISING A MEETING

- AGENDA
- LENGTH OF MEETING
- TYPE OF ROOM

B   WHAT IS IMPORTANT WHEN . . .?

ARRANGING ENTERTAINMENT FOR CLIENTS

- TYPE OF ACTIVITY
- VENUE
- COST

PART 3

Discussion – about 5 minutes

In this part of the test the examiner reads out a scenario and gives you some prompt material in the form of pictures or words. You have 30 seconds to look at the prompt card, an example of which is below, and then about 2 minutes to discuss the scenario with your partner. After that the examiner will ask you more questions related to the topic.

For **two** or **three** candidates

Scenario

I'm going to describe a situation.

A company is planning a recruitment day and is inviting students to look round. Talk together for about 2 minutes about the things the company could organise and decide together which 3 things would be the most useful.

Here are some ideas to help you.

Prompt material

- refreshments
- a guided tour
- promotional video
- free samples
- displays of products/services
- welcome speech
- free transport
- presentations

KEY

Test 1   Reading

Part 1

1 A   2 C   3 C   4 B   5 B

Part 2

6 B   7 G   8 A   9 H   10 E

Part 3

11 D   12 F   13 B   14 E   15 A

Part 4

16 B   17 B   18 C   19 A   20 A
21 C   22 A

Part 5

23 B   24 A   25 C   26 C   27 A
28 B

Part 6

29 A   30 C   31 B   32 B   33 C
34 C   35 B   36 A   37 A   38 B
39 B   40 C

Part 7

41 Collins Ltd   42 Sue Potts
43 7 Dawson Street   44 25(th) January
45 Radio advertisement/advert/ad

Test 1   Writing

Part 1

To: All staff
There will be an urgent meeting about our new
product at 10 am tomorrow in the new conference
room. I hope you can all come on time.

Part 2

Dear Mr Biggs
I am writing to accept your invitation. I am going
to talk about the new economy. I would like to
know how long the talk should be, so that I can
prepare it.

Concerning accommodation, could you help me
with booking? I would be very grateful.
Thank you for your invitation.
I look forward to seeing you again.
Yours sincerely
Celia Silva

Test 1   Listening

Part 1

1 B   2 B   3 A   4 B   5 A   6 C
7 A   8 C

Part 2

 9 Farrow   10 TM30096   11 24
12 15   13 2487   14 845   15 30(th)

Part 3

16 bank clerk
17 (financial) reports
18 hi(gh) (-) tech
19 lower charges
20 risk(s)
21 (new) offices
22 (a) team

Part 4

23 B   24 A   25 A   26 C
27 B   28 B   29 C   30 B

Tapescript

Listening Test One

*This is the Business English Certificate
Preliminary Level, Listening Test 1.*

Part One. Questions 1 to 8.

*For questions 1–8 you will hear 8 short
recordings. For each question, mark one letter (A,
B or C) for the correct answer.*

*Here is an example: When were the machine parts
sent?*

[pause]

Key

Woman: Mr Hooper rang. He needs those parts for the packing machine by the third.
Man: Well, it's already the first today . . . but wait . . . no, it's OK. They were sent out on the thirty-first.
Woman: Good. He'll certainly get them by the third, then.

[pause]

The answer is A.

Now we are ready to start.

After you have listened once, replay each recording.

[pause]

One: What time is the man's flight?

[pause]

Man: Sue, could you change my flight reservation for me? I've got an appointment in the morning so I won't be able to leave until after midday.
Woman: Yes, of course. What about the 1.15 flight? You'll get in at 3.30, so you'll be in time for the evening meeting.
Man: Thanks – that sounds great.

[pause]

Two: Which is the company's new packaging design?

[pause]

Woman: . . . so we're going to change our packaging in April, is that right?
Man: Yes, it's goodbye to the old white packets, with the two letter 'A's on them.
Woman: Right, and the new style?
Man: Well, we're going to have just a single 'A', in black on a grey packet, but with the same style writing.
Woman: Oh, that sounds good.

[pause]

Three: In which part of the month were sales the highest?

[pause]

Man: Our sales figures were quite good last month. They reached a peak in the first week, then they began to fall off towards the middle of the month, but they were already beginning to recover before the month ended.

[pause]

Four: Who does Brian Fry work for now?

Man: Welcome, everyone. I'd like to introduce Brian Fry, formerly chairman of ANK Oil and recently appointed President of the PTI. Many of you will know him best, of course, from when he was a government minister.

[pause]

Five: What is the man going to order?

[pause]

Man: Hello, Peggy, here are the catalogues I borrowed yesterday.
Woman: Oh, thanks, Sam. Did you find a filing cabinet you liked?
Man: Yes, this one . . . I'm going to phone the order through now. I like the desks as well – I don't need a new one, unfortunately!
Woman: And what about the computer chairs?
Man: Yes, they look really comfortable. Maybe another time!

[pause]

Six: What is the reduction in the company's exports?

[pause]

Man: The sales figures aren't good, are they?
Woman: No. Down by 8%. Exports are the problem . . . they're down by about 9% because interest rates have gone up again and the pound is so high.
Woman: So what are interest rates now?
Man: 7%, I hope they don't go up again.

[pause]

Seven: Where will the woman meet the visitors?

[pause]

Woman: You know these people who want to write about the company?
Man: Yes. You're meeting them next week, aren't you?
Woman: Mmm . . . Where should I take them? The factory perhaps?
Man: I suppose you'd prefer this office, because it's more comfortable?
Woman: Well, I did think here, yes or maybe a restaurant somewhere.
Man: I think they'd prefer to see where our products are made.
Woman: OK.

[pause]

Eight: What does the woman want the man to do?

[pause]

Woman: This photocopier's gone wrong again Bill. I think someone's used the wrong paper.
Man: Shall I call the engineer?
Woman: Well, I'll see if I can fix it myself first. But could you do a notice about the paper?

[pause]

That is the end of Part One.

[pause]

Part Two. Questions 9 to 15.

Look at the notes below.

Some information is missing.

You will hear a man telephoning a company about his statement of account.

For each question, 9–15, fill in the missing information in the numbered space using a word, numbers or letters.

After you have listened once, replay the recording.

You now have 10 seconds to look at the notes.

[pause]

Now listen, and write the missing information in the spaces.

Woman: Finance Department.
Man: Hello, I'm calling from the Pegasus Group. I've just received our statement of account and there are some problems.
Woman: I'll need to check our records. Can you give me your name?
Man: Martin Farrow – that's F A double R O W.
Woman: And your account number? It's at the top of your statement.
Man: It's TM 30096.
Woman: And what was wrong?
Man: We ordered 28 printers about two weeks ago but you only had 24 in stock so that was all you could deliver to us.
Woman: Were you charged for 28?
Man: No, but you hadn't included the correct discount. When I spoke to Sales we agreed a 15% reduction. On our statement it's 12%.
Woman: I'll look into it. The balance is wrong as well?

Man: Yes. It's £2,575 but that's with a 12% discount. It should be £2,487.
Woman: Can I check your phone number? In the records it's 840679 extension 854.
Man: The extension's 845.
Woman: I may need to ring back but we'll get a new statement posted this afternoon.
Man: Fine. Then I can sort out the payment. If the statement arrives tomorrow – that's the 15th – you should get the cheque by the end of the month on the 30th.
Woman: That'll be fine.

[pause]

Now listen to the recording again.

[pause]

That is the end of Part Two. You now have 10 seconds to check your answers.

[pause]

Part Three. Questions 16–22.

Look at the notes below.

Some information is missing.

You will hear Peter Dudley, Chief Executive of the Thorpe Group, giving a talk about his work to a group of business students.

For each question, 16–22, fill in the missing information in the numbered space using one or two words.

After you have listened once, replay the recording.

You now have 10 seconds to look at the notes.

[pause]

Now listen, and complete the notes.

Man: I've been Chief Executive of the Thorpe Group for eight years now. I started my career as a bank clerk but I later trained as an accountant. I suppose in one way or another, I've had a lot of experience of the financial side of business.

Nowadays it's my job to know what's happening in the market so every day at work I have financial reports to read. I only get the chance to look at other things – for example business magazines – when I travel abroad.

We invest customers' money in many areas of the market. Traditionally we've invested in property and in manufacturing. However, an industry that is doing very well at the moment is high-tech companies so we plan to increase investment in that area.

Some of our competitors concentrate on achieving a friendly service. This is important but I think that, on the whole, our customers prefer lower charges which is what we guarantee.

Although we encourage our staff to achieve a maximum return on investments, we have strict procedures to make sure that risks are avoided where possible. Some companies may put profits first but it's important that our customers see us as a safe investment.

Next month The Thorpe Group will merge with Chartwell Associates which means our company will be relocating to new offices. Most things, however, won't change – for example we won't lose any staff and there are no plans to invest in different areas of the market.

We are a market leader because of our experienced staff. When we take on staff we look for people who will perform well in a team. Since we train staff in many of the skills they need, a financial background is not essential.

[pause]

Now listen to the recording again.

[pause]

That is the end of Part Three. You now have 20 seconds to check your answers.

[pause]

Part Four. Questions 23–30.

You will hear a conversation between two employees of a company which is going to move its premises.

For each question 23–30, mark one letter (A, B or C) for the correct answer.

After you have listened once, replay the recording.

You now have 45 seconds to read through the questions.

[pause]

Now listen. Mark A, B or C.

Woman: John – I've just heard the company is moving out of these offices. I can't believe it!
Man: It's true. They made the final decision yesterday.
Woman: Who did?

Man: Um well . . .
Woman: There wasn't a board meeting yesterday, was there?
Man: I don't think so. A vote was actually taken by all the heads of departments.
Woman: Ah so it wasn't just Finance saying what should happen. It usually is . . . And where are we going? I like it here. I don't want to move my whole family to a new city none of us knows.
Man: You won't have to. We're not moving far away. We're only going to Kenton . . .
Woman: Kenton?
Man: You know, that new development. You must have noticed all the new building work going on, off the main road just as you come into the city.
Woman: Oh yes I've read about it. Is everyone who works here going, do you know, John?
Man: Almost everyone, you know, Finance, Sales, Public Relations . . .
Woman: Aha, so I will be going.
Man: Yes, though Customer Services are staying in the city centre for another year . . .
Woman: . . . so the public know where we are . . .
Man: Exactly. Fiona, it's going to be great. It's going to be much better there.
Woman: In what way? There'll be a better place for us to have lunch, I hope. The food here is getting worse every day.
Man: I don't know about that. But from what I've seen, there's going to be a lot more space than we've got at the moment and more rooms where we can have meetings.
Woman: Nice. And some sports facilities would be a good idea wouldn't they?
Man: They would but not at the moment, I'm afraid.
Woman: Oh well. Won't this move cost a lot of money?
Man: Why should it? I think the idea is to *save* money.
Woman: Are the offices in a new building or an old one?
Man: Oh, it's completely new, but it won't cost nearly as much as the rent on these city centre offices.
Woman: Oh. Are we getting new office furniture, then, to go in this new building?
Man: We are, someone's designing it specially but even that isn't really expensive. What *is* expensive is investing in new computers. Everything is going to be totally up to date.
Woman: Ooh, now that sounds exciting.

Man: It does, doesn't it? Actually, there's only one thing that worries me about the move.

Woman: What's that? Being the only business out at Kenton?

Man: Other firms'll soon join us when they see how cheap it is in Kenton. Actually, it's those of us without cars that might have a problem. I don't think there is much of a bus service. It's something the company will have to look at.

Woman: And what about shops? A lot of staff like going to the shops in the lunch hour.

Man: Well there are definitely some in Kenton.

Woman: Good!

Man: Actually, Fiona, there is one other rather interesting thing about this move. A lot of people are going over to new working contracts.

Woman: What! And what does that mean exactly? Does it mean we all lose our permanent contracts?

Man: It doesn't, actually. In this case it means people *can* set up a sort of office in their home if their work is suitable.

Woman: Uh huh. So it doesn't mean we have to work longer hours, or something?

Man: I don't think so.

Woman: John, you seem to know a lot about it. Are you in charge of arranging everything?

Man: I'm very happy to tell you it's someone else's job. All I've got to do is inform people about the move . . .

Woman: Mmm – you're doing very well.

Man: . . . except questions about contracts, hours and so on, of course.

Woman: Well, the Personnel Department does that, don't they?

Man: Exactly. And now I must get on . . .

[pause]

Now listen to the recording again.

[pause]

That is the end of Part Four. You now have ten minutes to transfer your answers to your Answer Sheet. Stop here and time ten minutes.

Test 2   Reading

Part 1

1 A   2 C   3 C   4 B   5 A

Part 2

6 G   7 A   8 B   9 C   10 F

Part 3

11 G   12 D   13 A   14 H   15 F

Part 4

16 B   17 C   18 B   19 A   20 B
21 C   22 A

Part 5

23 C   24 B   25 C   26 A   27 B
28 A

Part 6

29 A   30 C   31 B   32 B   33 A
34 C   35 B   36 B   37 C   38 C
39 A   40 B

Part 7

41 Bob Young   42 warehouse assistant
43 (Doctor / Dr. / J / Jake) Parry
44 broken arm
45 fortnight / two weeks

Test 2   Writing

Part 1

I have ordered some new PCs and monitors. Unfortunately the monitors will arrive in the second week of October. I apologise to the people who are waiting for a monitor.

Part 2

Dear Madam
I am writing to inform you that I would like to book from April 21 to April 22. In the conference, there will be 45 participants. Besides, I would like 20 single rooms with bathroom accommodation. I would like to have 46 computers, a fax machine, and a printer.
Please, let me know the cost of the weekend.
I look forward to hearing from you soon.
Yours faithfully
Lilian Lorten

Test 2   Listening

Part 1

1 B   2 C   3 C   4 A   5 B
6 B   7 C   8 A

Part 2

9 1976   10 118 million   11 54
12 Mackintosh   13 120,000
14 7,500   15 76

Part 3

16 racing car   17 low profits
18 1997   19 new equipment
20 chief executive   21 British
22 (an) electronics

Part 4

23 B   24 B   25 A   26 B   27 C
28 A   29 C   30 B

Tapescript

Listening Test Two

This is the Business English Certificate Preliminary Level, Listening Test 2.

Part One. Questions 1 to 8.

For questions 1–8 you will hear 8 short recordings. For each question, mark one letter (A, B or C) for the correct answer.

Here is an example: When were the machine parts sent?

[pause]

Woman: Mr Hooper rang. He needs those parts for the packing machine by the third.
Man: Well, it's already the first today . . . but wait . . . no, it's OK. They were sent out on the thirty-first.
Woman: Good. He'll certainly get them by the third, then.

[pause]

The answer is A.

Now we are ready to start.

After you have listened once, replay each recording.

[pause]

One: In which month will the auditors come?

[pause]

Woman: The auditors have rung to ask which month you'd prefer them to come, November or December?

Man: Why not September, like last year?
Woman: Somebody's already booked them for then, I'm afraid.
Man: November then. December's much too busy.

[pause]

Two: Which products have sold best?

[pause]

Woman: Now, let me turn to this month's sales figures . . . they're very mixed. Sales of fax machines are down again, but we've been doing quite *well* with answering machines. Mobile phones have been disappointing, though we're hoping they may improve with the new model coming out next month.

[pause]

Three: Where was the flight delayed?

[pause]

Man: Has the flight from Sydney arrived yet?
Woman: No, sir. It was held up in Singapore.
Man: Really? I thought it was a direct flight.
Woman: No, it stops in Bangkok and Hong Kong as well.

[pause]

Four: When are they going to meet?

[pause]

Woman 1: Could we meet on Thursday to discuss the new plans?
Woman 2: Sorry, I'm busy all day – how about Wednesday or Friday?
Woman 1: It'll have to be Wednesday – I'm going away on Friday.

[pause]

Five: Who will arrive late at the meeting?

[pause]

Woman: Oh, Mr Smith, before you go . . . I need to send out the agenda for Monday's meeting . . . who will be there?
Man: Er, John Brown from Sales will be there, and so will Mary Jones from Purchasing . . . But I know she'll be a bit late.
Woman: Who will be there from Production? Peter Wilson? He's back from holiday now.
Man: Yes, he'll be there.
Woman: Thanks, Mr Smith . . .

[pause]

Six: What does the annual report show about sales of clothes?

[pause]

Woman 1: We were expecting some loss of business this year, but I've just looked at the annual report, and I see sales have remained steady.
Woman 2: So, no change then?
Woman 1: Only in the *pattern* of sales. Men's clothes are our biggest earner now, about 50% of the total. Women's and children's clothes are selling equally well.

[pause]

Seven: Which flight is the man going to take to Paris?

[pause]

Man: Are you going to the Paris conference tomorrow?
Woman: Yes, I'm leaving here straight after the meeting with Bob at a quarter past twelve. My plane leaves at half-past two.
Man: Um, I was going to get the one o'clock flight, but I think perhaps I should be at Bob's meeting too. I'll get the same flight as you then.

[pause]

Eight: Which is the cheapest model?

[pause]

Woman: Let me also show you the Wilton and Asset models. Both are smaller and lighter than the Romex.
Man: But aren't they more expensive?
Woman: Well, they do actually cost a little more. But they're more efficient machines. And probably better value for money in the long term.

[pause]

That is the end of Part One.

[pause]

Part Two. Questions 9–15.

Look at the notes below.

Some information is missing.

You will hear an interview between Anna Marsh, who works for a business magazine, and Jim

Davenport, who works in the publicity department of a company, Gold Express.

For each question 9–15, fill in the missing information in the numbered space using a word, numbers or letters.

After you have listened once, replay the recording.

You now have 10 seconds to look at the notes.

[pause]

Now listen, and write the missing information in the spaces.

Man: Gold Express. Jim Davenport.
Woman: Morning. This is Anna Marsh from Business Review. You said you'd give me some information for the article I'm doing on delivery companies.
Man: Ah yes . . .
Woman: So, when did 'Gold Express' start doing business?
Man: Well, it had been in business for 10 years when I joined it in 1986, so that means it was set up in 1976.
Woman: I see. And what's your annual turnover?
Man: £118 million last year – that's £12 million more than the year before.
Woman: That's fantastic.
Man: Most similar companies have only grown by 8 to 9% in the last 5 years, but our business has grown by 54% in that time. I think that's due to our MD, Peter Mackintosh. That's spelled M-A-C-K-I-N-T-O-S-H. He's done a great job.
Woman: What ideas has he brought to the company?
Man: Well, first a very positive attitude to customer opinion. We have 120,000 customers, and we send questionnaires to 4,000 of those every 8 weeks.
Woman: That must be very useful for you.
Man: And we encourage all our staff – there are 7,500 now, because we've taken on another 450 this year – to give opinions too.
    Last month 76% of staff said they were 'totally satisfied' with their work here – that's 10% more than last time!
Woman: That's great, thanks.

[pause]

Now listen to the recording again.

[pause]

Key

That is the end of Part Two. You now have 10 seconds to check your answers.

[pause]

Part Three. Questions 16–22.

Look at the notes below.

Some information is missing.

You will hear part of a business news programme.

For each question 16–22, fill in the missing information in the numbered space using one or two words.

After you have listened once, replay the recording.

You now have 10 seconds to look at the notes.

[pause]

Now listen, and complete the notes.

Woman: And now here is the main business news of the day.

The UK company Waymans confirmed today that managers there were continuing to reorganise the company, and have now decided which of their businesses to sell. Both their car components business and their sports car production will stay within the company. However, the sale of their racing car business is planned for next month and already has a possible buyer. A spokesman for Waymans said the company had agreed to sell the business because of its low profits, even though sales which were poor last year have started to recover. The buyers are specialists in the field and are confident they can continue this recovery. Waymans' Director John Blake confirmed that the sale was just one of several major changes they had made in the company in 1999, a process started two years before, in 1997, by their MD. Mr Blake explained that having fewer businesses would leave more money available. It is believed that the company will spend any money made from next month's sale on new equipment, instead of the building work that was originally planned.

Man: Teltalk, the mobile phone company, today confirmed that David Driver is moving from his position as Personnel Director to become Chief Executive. Reports suggest he will take up the position next month. Earlier in the year Mr Driver announced that Teltalk might merge with a company in Europe, but latest reports are that they now intend to join a British company.

Teltalk has also announced that Greens, the software retailers, intend to sell their eleven per cent share in the company next month. Teltalk has not named the company which intends to buy this share but has confirmed that it is an electronics company.

[pause]

Now listen to the recording again.

[pause]

That is the end of Part Three. You now have 20 seconds to check your answers.

[pause]

Part Four. Questions 23–30.

You will hear an interview with a woman who publishes magazines.

For each question 23–30, mark one letter (A, B or C) for the correct answer.

After you have listened once, replay the recording.

You have 45 seconds to read through the questions.

[pause]

Now listen and mark A, B or C.

Man: I'd like to introduce our studio guest, Sally Upton, who was the editor of the magazine 'Teenage Fashion' and is now about to produce her own magazines. Welcome Sally.
Woman: Thank you.
Man: Sally, your first idea for publishing needed a one billion pound loan, didn't it?
Woman: It did. I wanted to buy MPC – the biggest magazine company in the UK. And the bank agreed!
Man: But in fact that deal didn't succeed, so you didn't borrow the money.
Woman: That's right. Someone made them a better offer and then not long after I just missed another deal with a smaller company. So, in the end I decided to see if it would be possible to find finance for a completely new company, which I've called Close Communications.
Man: Was it easy to find a bank to agree to the idea of a new company?

Woman: It's harder to get financial support for starting a new company than for buying an existing one, even though I didn't want nearly as much as a billion pounds. I tried a lot of bankers, but none wanted to invest in us.

Man: So, what then?

Woman: Well, I got a business partner, and he suggested something really simple. We rang up six friends we knew had money to invest, and asked them to support us, and they agreed!

Man: Well, they *were* good friends! And how did you recruit your staff? I've heard you use quite unusual methods . . .

Woman: We didn't have to advertise formally in newspapers, in fact people contacted *us*, not us *them*. We asked them out for dinner to discuss their ideas and if we liked what they said, we asked them to be on the team.

Man: So in general do you see your company as being different to most other companies?

Woman: In every way – big and small. Take company transport policy. We don't have company cars, we don't think they make sense. In fact I come in by bicycle.

Man: Really?

Woman: However, we do give our employees a very generous expense account for rail journeys – it doesn't matter what the distance is, we are happy to pay the fare! Just so the team get out and meet people.

Man: And do you think you will stay different? Will success change you?

Woman: Not at all! For example, if Close Communications is successful, all the staff will benefit, because we are all equals. We don't give large rises in salary or extra pay every now and again but we do have a division of the profits every three months.

Man: I see.

Woman: Also, when we moved into our office we wanted everyone to feel at home. We didn't want everyone to have the same desks and chairs like a school or even to choose from a narrow range. So, to get it furnished, we gave them the money and let them choose exactly what they wanted.

Man: Brave.

Woman: Not brave. We trust each other! You see, I think there's only one reason why anybody becomes unhappy at work . . .

Man: What's that?

Woman: Well, in my experience it's not pay, it's

when you're not allowed to make any decisions because you always have to do what the managers say. Your voice isn't heard.

Man: Personally, it's filling in forms and filing papers that I hate most.

Woman: Yes, but they're *your* papers, it's different isn't it?

Man: True. And now the big day has come, your own magazines produced by your own company. Your first two titles tomorrow, both aimed at girls under 16, is that right?

Woman: That's right, they are just two of the nine we are going to produce in our first twelve months.

Man: Well, Sally, best of luck to you and your team tomorrow.

Woman: Thank you.

Man: And now . . .

[pause]

Now listen to the recording again.

[pause]

That is the end of Part Four. You now have ten minutes to transfer your answers to your Answer Sheet. Stop here and time ten minutes.

Test 3 Reading

Part 1

| 1 C | 2 C | 3 A | 4 B | 5 B |

Part 2

| 6 F | 7 G | 8 A | 9 H | 10 E |

Part 3

| 11 A | 12 D | 13 F | 14 B | 15 G |

Part 4

| 16 A | 17 B | 18 A | 19 C | 20 B |
| 21 C | 22 A |

Part 5

| 23 C | 24 C | 25 A | 26 B | 27 C |
| 28 A |

Part 6

29 B	30 C	31 A	32 B	33 C
34 C	35 B	36 B	37 A	38 A
39 B	40 C

Part 7

41 Northern Software   42 24 Queens Road
43 EV311   44 white   45 next day

Test 3   Writing

Part 1

I'm coming to New York office on 3 February to the meeting. Is it possible to start at 11:00 am? After that, would you like to have dinner with me?

Part 2

Dear Mary
Thank you for your invite to your new Head Office. I want to tell you the number of participants for the visit will be 20 people.
My colleague and I would like to see the Financial Department and also the Sales Department, and naturally the IT Department.
I would like also to know the time for the visit.
Best wishes
Pim Schuler

Test 3   Listening

Part 1

1 C   2 C   3 B   4 A   5 B   6 B
7 C   8 B

Part 2

9 11.29 (am)   10 227   11 B 38
12 (£)190   13 15a   14 LPD662
15 Mary Hallett

Part 3

16 (old) airport
17 14(th) March
18 retail outlet
19 (car) tyres/tires
20 (a) repair service
21 training
22 conference centre

Part 4

23 C   24 B   25 C   26 A
27 B   28 C   29 A   30 B

Tapescript

Listening Test Three

This is the Business English Certificate Preliminary Level, Listening Test 3.

Part One. Questions 1 to 8.

For questions 1–8 you will hear 8 short recordings. For each question, mark one letter (A, B or C) for the correct answer.

Here is an example: When were the machine parts sent?

[pause]

Woman: Mr Hooper rang. He needs those parts for the packing machine by the third.
Man: Well, it's already the first today . . . but wait . . . no, it's OK. They were sent out on the thirty-first.
Woman: Good. He'll certainly get them by the third, then.

[pause]

The answer is A.

Now we are ready to start.

After you have listened once, replay each recording.

[pause]

One: Where is the Emerald Airlines office?

[pause]

Woman: Good morning. Emerald Airlines!
Man: Er . . . hello, I've got to get to your office. Can I walk there? I'm at the station.
Woman: Oh yes. Turn right out of the station, walk to the end of the road, then turn left. It's the building on your right, opposite the park.
Man: Thanks.

[pause]

Two: When will they deliver the new computer?

[pause]

Woman: Hello, it's Ace Computers. Your new computer is ready – could we deliver it early next week – say, on the third of May?
Man: Mmm. Well, on the second and third I'll be away at a conference.
Woman: Would the fourth be convenient?
Man: Yes, that should be OK. Thanks.

[pause]

Three: Which chart shows foreign trade this year?

[pause]

. . . and, although at present 25% of our trade is done abroad, this should increase by 10% next year. We plan to expand foreign trade to 50% of our market within three years.

[pause]

Four: Which product does the man still need?

[pause]

Man: It's Derek Bond from Robinsons Ltd here. I'm phoning about my order for office equipment. I received the floppy disks last Monday, but the pens I ordered were missing, and they weren't with the copying paper that arrived yesterday.

[pause]

Five: What is Helen's degree in?

[pause]

Woman 1: Helen, I've typed your CV . . . for the application for that management job.
Woman 2: Oh right, thanks . . . I'll check it . . . mm, yes, that looks OK. Oh . . . actually, my degree wasn't in management . . .
Woman 1: Oh sorry, what was it, then?
Woman 2: . . . languages . . . and then perhaps you could add my computer skills diploma as well. That's *very* important.

[pause]

Six: How much per metre will the woman pay?

[pause]

Woman: I'm ringing about your quotation for the grey wool cloth. £6.50 a metre seems a bit high to me. You supplied a similar one to us at £5.95 recently.
Man: Yes, but you took 60 metres that time. I can come down to £6.15 if you can order 50 metres.
Woman: OK. Thanks.

[pause]

Seven: Who are the speakers?

[pause]

Woman: Good morning, Mr Garcia.
Man: Hello, Mrs Moore. How nice to see you . . . and what a pleasure to welcome you to Oak

Valley Foods again. I think you'll be glad you came to see us today . . . we have an exciting range of soft drinks to show you, and I think you'll find the prices very reasonable.

[pause]

Eight: Which chart is correct?

[pause]

Woman: Right. So now we come to the sales figures. What are they like, Jack?
Man: Well, I'm afraid they're lower than in 97. Those figures were very high, and there's been a big fall in demand since then . . .

[pause]

That is the end of Part One.

[pause]

Part Two. Questions 9–15.

Look at the notes below.

You will hear a woman booking a train ticket.

For each question 9–15, fill in the missing information in the numbered space using a word, numbers or letters.

After you have listened once, replay the recording.

You now have 10 seconds to look at the notes.

[pause]

Now listen, and write the missing information in the spaces.

Man: Eurotrains. How can I help you?
Woman: Hello. I'm calling from Dent Ltd. I need to book a Paris ticket for one of our managers, for tomorrow.
Man: Oh yes. At what time?
Woman: His meeting's at 3pm, so arriving some time before then – perhaps 2.30?
Man: Hmm, the best I could do is one getting in at fourteen twenty which leaves at eleven twenty-nine – would that do?
Woman: Yes, OK. Can you reserve that, for Clive Black?
Man: Black . . . sure. That train's the two-two-seven. It's the non-stop express. Will that be in First Class?
Woman: Yes, and forward-facing.
Man: So, First Class is in Coach B, second from the front, and it'll be seat 38.

Woman: Right. Can you charge our account in the usual way? I think it's something like £170, isn't it?

Man: Actually, there's a surcharge on the non-stop trains, so it'll come to £190 this time.

Woman: OK.

Man: Can you ask Mr Black to collect his ticket and check in no later than 11 o'clock at desk 15a?

Woman: Sure. Is there a reservation number or something he'll need?

Man: Mmm, it's L P D double 6 2.

Woman: And your name, in case there's any problem?

Man: Well, I'm David Gress, but I'm not in tomorrow, so you'd need to ask for Mary Hallett – that's H-A-double-L-E-double-T.

Woman: Thanks very much . . .

[pause]

Now listen to the recording again.

[pause]

That is the end of Part Two. You now have 10 seconds to check your answers.

[pause]

Part Three. Questions 16–22.

Look at the notes below.

Some information is missing.

You will hear Alan French, the Managing Director of A2Z Racing, talking at a public meeting about his future plans.

For each question, 16–22, fill in the missing information in the numbered space using one or two words.

After you have listened once, replay the recording.

You now have 10 seconds to look at the notes.

[pause]

Now listen, and complete the notes

Man: Good evening everyone. My name's Alan French, and I'm the managing director of A2Z Racing. Thanks for inviting me to speak to you about the development of the new racetrack here in Bramford. The plan is to build it on the site of the old airport behind the new leisure centre. It was reported in the local paper that we were going to start work on 4th April, but in fact it'll now be on the 14th of March.

The total cost of the project will be around £4 million, and we have as our partners in this project SPC, the sports clothes manufacturers, who will open a retail outlet and 'sports café' on the site. They're well-known for the high quality of their goods and competitive prices, so I'm certain they'll do well. The producer of car tyres, Runwells, have also joined us. They will offer a repair service to both the general public and the racing industry. We are therefore confident that the new 10km track and the other businesses related to it will bring increased employment opportunities to the area.

You may also be pleased to hear that the track will be used for racing just twice a month, so there should be no problem with noise. At other times the police and ambulance service will use it for training purposes. Of course, my own racing team will practise there.

We aim to attract as many people as possible, and in addition to the excellent facilities I've already mentioned we are hoping to provide local businesses with a conference centre in a few years' time. Now . . . if you have any questions, I'll be pleased to answer them.

[pause]

Now listen to the recording again.

[pause]

That is the end of Part Three. You now have 20 seconds to check your answers.

[pause]

Part Four. Questions 23–30.

You will hear a discussion between a radio interviewer and the owners of two companies which sell sandwiches.

For each question, 23–30, mark one letter (A, B or C) for the correct answer.

After you have listened once, replay the recording.

You now have 45 seconds to read through the questions.

[pause]

Now listen, and mark A, B or C.

Interviewer: Well, today on Starting Out, we look at the sandwich industry in Britain. I have with me Brian Fraser, the owner of 'Designer Sandwiches', and Geraldine Holmes, another successful sandwich shop owner from Brighton. Brian did you have any problems developing your business?

Brian Fraser: Not at the start. I set up my first sandwich shop in Leeds in 1994. That went well. Unfortunately, though, just before the opening of my second shop, there was a fire in the empty building. So I had to start again and find new premises for it. It's doing as well as the first one now, though.

Interviewer: Why do you think you have been so successful?

Brian Fraser: There's a high demand for sandwiches made from fresh ingredients, especially when they're served in a relaxed and friendly place. Although people have a bit less time nowadays, they're still happy to pay more for something really good.

Interviewer: Of course some people take your sandwiches straight back to their desks. Is that a growing trend?

Brian Fraser: Quite the opposite! It used to be true, but now, because many offices ban smoking completely, we find a lot of people stay at our tables and chat over a cigarette after their sandwich. No one wants to stand outside smoking, especially in winter, and because we're near their offices, people often come in twice a day.

Interviewer: So how long is the average lunch break nowadays?

Brian Fraser: It's nowhere near an hour, of course. I'm told it's slightly more than 30 minutes, I can't remember the exact figure, but well under forty minutes.

Interviewer: Designer Sandwiches are the perfect choice, then . . . if you're living in Leeds! Now Geraldine, how did you start your own business?

Geraldine Holmes: Well, it was by accident, really. I planned to train as a journalist, but I got an office job to earn some money first. There were no places to buy a cheap snack near where I worked. My colleagues used to complain about this. So I thought there's an excellent idea here and I made a start immediately.

Interviewer: And how did you finance the business when you started?

Geraldine Holmes: Well, you have to understand that I began in a very small way! So I really didn't need a loan from the bank. I used to fill a basket with about forty sandwiches, sell them in local offices, and, when the basket was empty,

make some more. The little money I'd saved bought the first ingredients, and after that, I always had cash coming in, so there was no need for my parents to help either.

Interviewer: Very low risk! Was it difficult to develop the business though?

Geraldine Holmes: Yes and no. I made a reasonable profit from the start, so I was able to afford to rent a small place. I sold my sandwiches there, but also continued to supply the many customers I already had. The problem was, I had to close the premises while I delivered to their various offices.

Interviewer: So then you employed Jack Roberts, now your business partner, to help you?

Geraldine Holmes: Employ, no! I couldn't afford wages. Jack had a very good job then, though he hated it. When I asked him to join the business, he seemed interested. Fortunately for me, he had two weeks off work at the time, so he agreed to take over the deliveries temporarily. Well, he enjoyed it so much, he decided to give up his proper job and take a risk with me.

Interviewer: And from then on, success was guaranteed! Geraldine Holmes, Brian Fraser, thank you for sharing your early careers with us.

[pause]

Now listen to the recording again.

[pause]

That is the end of Part Four. You now have ten minutes to transfer your answers to your Answer Sheet. Stop here and time ten minutes.

Test 4   Reading

Part 1

1 C   2 B   3 C   4 A   5 B

Part 2

6 G   7 E   8 D   9 B   10 A

Part 3

11 E   12 H   13 F   14 G   15 C

Part 4

16 B   17 C   18 B   19 A   20 B
21 C   22 A

Part 5

23 C	24 B	25 C	26 A	27 B
28 C				

Part 6

29 A	30 B	31 A	32 C	33 B
34 C	35 A	36 C	37 A	38 C
39 A	40 C			

Part 7

41 Star Employment   42 Mr Gordon
43 Recruitment Today
44 half page   45 £150

Test 4   Writing

Part 1

To: Human Resources Manager
From: John Jones
I'm attending a Conference in the USA next week
on 18th & 19th March and my PA is on leave so
could you arrange a temporary PA for the trip?
Thanks

Part 2

Fax to Sally Saunders

Dear Mrs Saunders
Thank you for your fax. I am afraid I confirm my
original dates for the conference because we
cannot move it to the following week.
I am going to book 20 twin-bedded rooms. About
the special menu – I would like some typical
dishes because most of the participants come from
other countries.
I look forward to hearing from you.
Your sincerely

Test 4   Listening

Part 1

1 B	2 A	3 C	4 C	5 B
6 C	7 B	8 C		

Part 2

9 Howlett   10 3   11 26(th)
12 8   13 (£)9.50   14 630097
15 Central

Part 3

16 1975
17 product quality/quality products
18 (new) computers/computer system
19 bonuses
20 funding/money/grants
21 attitude
22 marketing

Part 4

23 A	24 C	25 B	26 C
27 B	28 C	29 A	30 A

Tapescript

Listening Test Four

*This is the Business English Certificate
Preliminary Level, Listening Test 4.*

Part One. Questions 1 to 8.

*For questions 1–8 you will hear 8 short
recordings. For each question, mark one letter (A,
B or C) for the correct answer.*

*Here is an example: When were the machine parts
sent?*

[pause]

Woman: Mr Hooper rang. He needs those parts
for the packing machine by the third.
Man: Well, it's already the first today . . . but wait
. . . no, it's OK. They were sent out on the
thirty-first.
Woman: Good. He'll certainly get them by the
third, then.

[pause]

The answer is A.

Now we are ready to start.

*After you have listened once, replay each
recording.*

[pause]

*One: Which department has a vacancy at the
moment?*

[pause]

Man: Good morning. Maxton Products.
Woman: Oh, hello. I saw in the paper last week
that you've got a vacancy for a secretary in your
production department.

Man: Well, actually that vacancy was in the personnel department but the position's filled now. We are looking for a secretary in the sales department, though.

Woman: Thanks, but I'm not really interested . . .

[pause]

Two: How will Dover Tools dispatch the order?

[pause]

Man: Purchasing.

Woman: Dover Tools here. About your order – how would you like it sent?

Man: Well, road is probably cheapest, isn't it?

Woman: Yes, but it'll take 10 days . . . is there a rail depot near you?

Man: No there isn't . . . I suppose you'd better put it on the plane, then . . . it's urgent.

Woman: OK – We'll deliver in 48 hours. Does that suit you?

Man: Yes, that's OK.

[pause]

Three: What is the message for Mr Brown?

[pause]

Man: Hello, can I help you?

Woman: Hello, yes, my name's Jane Kelly. I'm looking for Mr Brown.

Man: Oh, I'm sorry he's not here . . . do you have an appointment?

Woman: No, I don't . . . I was just passing the factory, so I thought I'd come in and show him our new samples . . . never mind . . . tell him I called, and I'll come back another time.

Man: Fine, I'll give him your message.

[pause]

Four: When will production start?

[pause]

Man: – now – about the new factory. We *were* hoping to start production on the 21st . . . unfortunately it'll be about a week later now, on the 29th . . . the machinery won't be installed until the 23rd – that's why there's a delay, I'm afraid.

[pause]

Five: Which chart are the two women talking about?

[pause]

Woman 1: Look, we've got to do something about these sales figures – they're terrible!

Woman 2: Well, they're better than last month, anyway.

Woman 1: Yes, but not a lot. We can certainly still improve them. I'm getting very worried . . .

[pause]

Six: Which car park will close during repair work?

[pause]

Man: You know next week the factory chimneys are going to be repaired?

Woman: Yes.

Man: Well, we'll have to close the car park underneath the chimneys.

Woman: OK. That's the West Site car park . . . so West Site workers will have to use the East Site car park instead.

Man: Yes, or the North Site, if that's full.

[pause]

Seven: When are the two people going to meet?

[pause]

Woman: Hello, Edith Brown here, from Walkers. Could I make an appointment to see you on Thursday morning this week?

Man: Morning's not really possible, I'm afraid. What about the afternoon?

Woman: I've already got an appointment then. Is Friday possible?

Man: Yes, that's OK, but make it the morning rather than the afternoon.

[pause]

Eight: Which graph is correct?

[pause]

The price of shares remained steady for the first half of the year but there was a sudden fall in their value in the second half.

[pause]

That is the end of Part One.

Part Two. Questions 9 to 15.

Look at the notes below.

Some information is missing.

You will hear a man contacting an employment agency about the recruitment of temporary staff for his business.

For each question 9–15, fill in the missing information in the numbered space using a word, numbers or letters.

After you have listened once, replay the recording

You have now 10 seconds to look at the notes.

[pause]

Now listen, and write the missing information in the spaces.

Woman: Advance Recruitment.

Man: Hello, I'm phoning from A&T Computer Solutions. I was hoping you could help us with some temporary office staff.

Woman: Of course. Can I take your name please?

Man: It's John Howlett. That's H-O-W-L-E double T.

Woman: Fine. And what kind of posts are they?

Man: Well, we're looking for 3 secretaries. Two secretaries are leaving so we have to replace them but we're also very busy and need another secretary because of the extra work.

Woman: And when will they start?

Man: Our secretaries leave next Friday – the 23rd. So we'd like your people for the 26th – if that's possible.

Woman: It should be. And how long are the jobs for?

Man: At least 8 weeks. It may become as long as 12 but we'd only decide that 2 or 3 weeks after they'd started.

Woman: It's 40 hours a week?

Man: Yes. We normally pay £6.50 per hour to our permanent staff. What will you charge us?

Woman: For experienced secretaries it's £9.50 per hour.

Man: Right well we'd obviously need experienced staff.

Woman: Fine. Can I ring you back later?

Man: Yes, the number's 6 3 double 0 9 7 and my extension is 218.

Woman: Oh, one more thing. Where are the company offices?

Man: Central Business Park – on Broad Street.

Woman: Thank you.

[pause]

Now listen to the recording again.

[pause]

That is the end of Part Two. You now have 10 seconds to check your answers.

[pause]

Part Three. Questions 16 to 22.

Look at the notes below.

Some information is missing.

You will hear a management consultant giving a business studies lecture about MTF, a company that manufactures heating systems.

For each question 16–22, fill in the missing information in the numbered space using one or two words.

After you have listened once, replay the recording.

You now have 10 seconds to look at the notes.

[pause]

Now listen, and complete the notes.

[pause]

Woman: I'm going to talk today about MTF, a firm in the North of England that manufactures heating systems. It was set up by David Ross, an engineer who had previously worked in car manufacturing. When David lost his job in 1974 he decided to set up his own company and this opened for business in 1975. It proved very successful and the company now has a turnover of 12.5 million.

In the early days, Ross rejected the idea of a competitive pricing policy to establish the company. He always thought that product quality was more important to the company's success. He believes this approach has helped make the company a market leader.

Five years ago the company bought new machinery. This has been a success and they now intend to spend large sums on a new computer system. This will improve the speed of customer service.

David Ross believes the workforce plays a large part in the success of his firm. There is a good relationship between management and staff. Basic pay is average for the area and holidays are standard but the company pays bonuses to staff when large orders are finished on time.

Local government wants to encourage training schemes in the workplace and MTF has successfully applied to them for funding. MTF hopes that the company's training scheme will increase productivity but they accept that money invested in training doesn't guarantee this.

MTF doesn't have a large management structure and it has promoted most of its managers from within the company. Ross does not believe management qualifications are important and looks instead for people with a positive attitude towards the company.

Ross believes his company can maintain its market position. He has invested a lot of money in the production process and is confident about the skills of his workforce. Marketing, however, is one part of the business he recognises could get better.

[pause]

Now listen to the lecture again.

[pause]

That is the end of Part Three. You have 20 seconds to check your answers.

[pause]

Part Four. Questions 23 to 30.

You will hear a radio interview with a representative of the New Zealand Kiwi fruit Marketing Board (the KMB), about the sale and export of kiwi fruit.

For each question 23–30, mark one letter (A, B or C) for the correct answer.

After you have listened once, replay the recording.

You have 45 seconds to read through the questions.

[pause]

Now listen and mark A, B or C.

Man 1: Good evening. On 'Business World' tonight, it's my pleasure to welcome Peter Bull from the New Zealand Kiwi Fruit Marketing Board – the KMB for short! Good to have you with us, Peter. First of all, for those people who may not have seen kiwi fruit, what are they?

Man 2: Well, they're a small, green, round fruit and they're delicious! New Zealand now exports more of them than any other fruit and vegetable – so kiwi fruit are very important to us economically. Of course, New Zealand is famous for lamb and wool production, and trade in both of these is still very good – though *dairy products* is actually the biggest area in terms of export income.

Man 1: I see . . . and can you tell me why the KMB was started?

Man 2: Well, some years ago kiwi fruit farmers found they were producing more fruit, but the market wasn't growing at the same rate. So the KMB was formed – partly to set up distribution to retailers and so on within New Zealand, but also to find more customers for kiwi fruit around the world – in other words, to make the export market bigger.

Man 1: I see . . . now just what *do* you do to find more customers around the world for a particular product . . . especially one which people have probably never seen before?

Man 2: Well, there are a number of ways of doing this. Some marketing boards might do an international advertising campaign, so that when anybody in one of the target countries watches TV, they're certain to see the product. That's fine, but of course it costs a lot, and it's not really suited to our product. So we've always approached this in a different way – we want to be certain that anyone who buys our product anywhere in the world has a guarantee that what they're buying is of the highest quality. This is the best long-term policy . . . you can do all kinds of things, like selling at cost price at the beginning so that your product is cheaper than its competitors, but we didn't think that would present the right image, and in the end you'll only have to raise your prices anyway.

Man 1: So, as with anything, it all comes down to how good your product is . . .

Man 2: That's right.

Man 1: And where do most exports of kiwi fruit go?

Man 2: Well, our market is expanding all the time. Our oldest markets are in Europe and Japan, but demand is growing in the Middle East and Korea. Our latest destinations are South America and Vietnam.

Man 1: Really? So kiwi fruit are becoming truly international . . .

Man 2: Yes. And kiwi fruit currently make up 25% of all fruit exported by New Zealand.

Man 1: And do you expect that to rise?

Man 2: Yes – to 32% in five years' time, a 7% increase we hope!

Man 1: Mmm – OK how does the fruit get from grower to customer?

Man 2: Well, most kiwi is exported by sea though some is sent by air freight to Australia. The fruit comes into the ports by truck, after being packed by the growers at local packing stations.

There is a plan for express rail transport in the future, which should speed things up a bit more.

Man 1: And after the fruit arrives at the ports?

Man 2: Well, it's stored on the ships in large wooden boxes. We send 50 million boxes out of the country on 80 ships – but that's not enough! We're quite happy with the design of the boxes, and we know we've got exactly the right temperature on board for the fruit – in other words, our technology isn't a problem – we simply need more ships to be able to work as efficiently as we'd like to.

Man 1: And how do you see the future developing?

Man 2: Well, we hope to work out ways to send the fruit even more quickly to our export markets, to keep it as fresh as possible.

Man 1: Mmm – well thank you, Peter. One last question – is kiwi fruit popular in New Zealand?

Man 2: Yes . . . In fact it recently became the second biggest seller on the home market. It's overtaken sales of pears – although it'll be a while yet before we overtake apples. But that's OK of course, because *all* New Zealand fruit is delicious!

[pause]

Now listen to the recording again.

[pause]

That is the end of Part Four. You now have ten minutes to transfer your answers to your Answer Sheet. Stop here and time ten minutes.

INTERLOCUTOR FRAMES

To facilitate practice for the Speaking test, the scripts that the interlocutor follows for Parts 2 and 3 appear below. They should be used in conjunction with Tests 1–4 Speaking tasks.

Interlocutor frames are not included for Part 1, in which the interlocutor asks the candidates questions directly rather than asking them to perform tasks.

PART 2: Mini presentations for 2 candidates (about 5 minutes)

Interlocutor:
- Thank you. That's the end of the first part of the test. In the next part you are each going to talk on your own.
- Now, I'm going to give each of you a card with two topics. I'd like you to choose one topic and talk about it for about one minute. You have one minute to prepare for this. You are allowed to make notes.
- All right? Here are your topics.

[Each candidate is handed a different topic card, and some paper and a pencil for notes.]

Interlocutor:
- Choose one of the topics and prepare to talk about it. Remember you can make notes if you wish.

[1 minute's preparation time. Both candidates prepare their talks at the same time, separately.]

Interlocutor:
- All right. Now, *B, which topic have you chosen, A or B? So would you like to talk about what you think is important when (xxx).

[B talks.]

Interlocutor:
- Thank you. Now, *A, which do you think is most important (xxx), (yyy), or (zzz)?

[A replies.]

- Thank you. All right. Now, *A, which topic have you chosen, A or B? So would you like to talk about what you think is important when (xxx).

[A talks.]

- Thank you. Now, *B, which do you think is most important (xxx), (yyy), or (zzz)?

[B replies.]

- Thank you.

[Materials are collected.]

*USE CANDIDATES' NAMES THROUGHOUT THE TEST

PART 3 : Collaborative task and discussion (about 5 minutes)

Interlocutor:
- Now, in this part of the test you are going to talk about something together.
- I'm going to describe a situation.

Example: A company is planning a recruitment day and is inviting students to look round. Talk together for about 2 minutes about the things the company could organise and decide together which 3 things would be the most useful.

- Here are some ideas to help you.

[Task sheet 1 is placed in front of the candidates so that they can both see it.]

Think about the ideas for a few seconds.
- I'll describe the situation again.

Example: A company is planning a recruitment day and is inviting students to look round. Talk together for about 2 minutes about the things the company could organise and decide together which 3 things would be the most useful.

Now talk together. Please speak so that we can hear you.

[Candidates have about 2 minutes to complete the task.]

[Materials are collected.]

[Interlocutor selects one or more of the following questions as appropriate.]

Example:
- Do you think it's useful for students to visit companies? (Why/Why not?)

123

- Which staff should help organise this type of event? (Why/Why not?)
- How useful are recruitment days for companies? (Why?)

- Would you enjoy helping to organise a recruitment day? (Why/Why not?)

- Thank you. That is the end of the Speaking test.

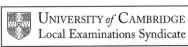
UNIVERSITY *of* CAMBRIDGE
Local Examinations Syndicate

PRELIMINARY

Candidate Name
If not already printed, write name in CAPITALS and complete the Candidate No. grid (in pencil).

Candidate's Signature

Examination Title

Centre

Supervisor:
If the candidate is ABSENT or has WITHDRAWN shade here ⬚

Centre No.

Candidate No.

Examination Details

0	0	0	0
1	1	1	1
2	2	2	2
3	3	3	3
4	4	4	4
5	5	5	5
6	6	6	6
7	7	7	7
8	8	8	8
9	9	9	9

BEC Preliminary Reading Answer Sheet

Instructions
Use a PENCIL (B or HB).
Rub out any answer you wish to change with an eraser.

For **Parts 1 to 6:**
Mark one box for each answer.

For example:
If you think C is the right answer to the question, mark your answer sheet like this:

0 | A B C

For **Part 7:**
Write your answer clearly in CAPITAL LETTERS.
Write one letter or number in each box.
If the answer has more than one word, leave one box empty between words.

For example:

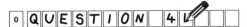
0 | Q U E S T I O N 4 |

Part 1		**Part 2**	
1	A B C	6	A B C D E F G H
2	A B C	7	A B C D E F G H
3	A B C	8	A B C D E F G H
4	A B C	9	A B C D E F G H
5	A B C	10	A B C D E F G H

Turn over for Parts 3 - 7 ▶

BEC P - R

DP453/353

Photocopiable © UCLES

125

Part 3

11	A	B	C	D	E	F	G	H
12	A	B	C	D	E	F	G	H
13	A	B	C	D	E	F	G	H
14	A	B	C	D	E	F	G	H
15	A	B	C	D	E	F	G	H

Part 4

16	A	B	C
17	A	B	C
18	A	B	C
19	A	B	C
20	A	B	C
21	A	B	C
22	A	B	C

Part 5

23	A	B	C
24	A	B	C
25	A	B	C
26	A	B	C
27	A	B	C
28	A	B	C

Part 6

29	A	B	C
30	A	B	C
31	A	B	C
32	A	B	C

33	A	B	C
34	A	B	C
35	A	B	C
36	A	B	C

37	A	B	C
38	A	B	C
39	A	B	C
40	A	B	C

Part 7

41

1 41 0

42

1 42 0

43

1 43 0

44

1 44 0

45

1 45 0

Photocopiable © UCLES

UNIVERSITY *of* **CAMBRIDGE**
Local Examinations Syndicate

PRELIMINARY

Candidate Name
If not already printed, write name
in CAPITALS and complete the
Candidate No. grid (in pencil).

Candidate Signature

Examination Title

Centre

Supervisor:
If the candidate is ABSENT or has WITHDRAWN shade here ⊂⊃

Centre No.

Candidate No.

Examination Details

0	0	0	0
1	1	1	1
2	2	2	2
3	3	3	3
4	4	4	4
5	5	5	5
6	6	6	6
7	7	7	7
8	8	8	8
9	9	9	9

BEC Preliminary Writing answer sheet

Part 1: Write your answer in the box below.

Write your answer to Part 2 on the other side of this sheet ▶

This section for use by Examiner only						
Part 1	0	1	2	3	4	5

BEC P - W

DP999/999

Photocopiable © UCLES

127

Part 2: Write your answer in the box below.

This section for use by Examiner only

Part 2	0	1.1	1.2	2.1	2.2	3.1	3.2	4.1	4.2	5.1	5.2

Examiner Number

$_c0_3$ $_c1_3$ $_c2_3$ $_c3_3$ $_c4_3$ $_c5_3$ $_c6_3$ $_c7_3$ $_c8_3$ $_c9_3$
$_c0_3$ $_c1_3$ $_c2_3$ $_c3_3$ $_c4_3$ $_c5_3$ $_c6_3$ $_c7_3$ $_c8_3$ $_c9_3$
$_c0_3$ $_c1_3$ $_c2_3$ $_c3_3$ $_c4_3$ $_c5_3$ $_c6_3$ $_c7_3$ $_c8_3$ $_c9_3$
$_c0_3$ $_c1_3$ $_c2_3$ $_c3_3$ $_c4_3$ $_c5_3$ $_c6_3$ $_c7_3$ $_c8_3$ $_c9_3$

Examiner's Signature

Photocopiable © UCLES

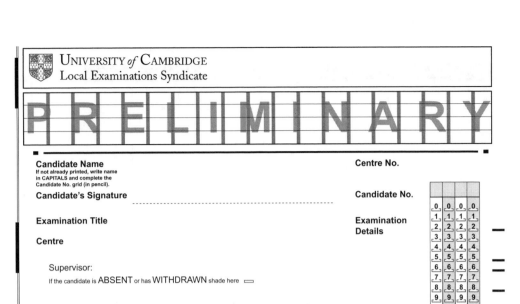

UNIVERSITY *of* CAMBRIDGE
Local Examinations Syndicate

PRELIMINARY

Candidate Name
If not already printed, write name in CAPITALS and complete the Candidate No. grid (in pencil).

Candidate's Signature

Examination Title

Centre

Supervisor:
If the candidate is ABSENT or has WITHDRAWN shade here ▭

Centre No.

Candidate No.

Examination Details

0	0	0	0
1	1	1	1
2	2	2	2
3	3	3	3
4	4	4	4
5	5	5	5
6	6	6	6
7	7	7	7
8	8	8	8
9	9	9	9

BEC Preliminary Listening Answer Sheet

Instructions
Use a PENCIL (B or HB).
Rub out any answer you wish to change with an eraser.

For **Parts 1 and 4:**
Mark one box for each answer.
For example:
If you think C is the right answer to the question, mark your answer sheet like this:

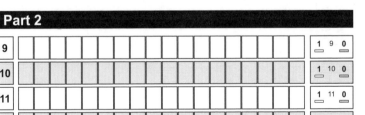

For **Parts 2 and 3:**
Write your answer clearly in CAPITAL LETTERS. Write one letter in each box.
If the answer has more than one word, leave one box empty between words.
For example:

| 0 | Y | O | U | R | | A | N | S | W | E | R | | |

Part 1

1	A	B	C
2	A	B	C
3	A	B	C
4	A	B	C
5	A	B	C
6	A	B	C
7	A	B	C
8	A	B	C

Part 2

9																1 9 0
10																1 10 0
11																1 11 0
12																1 12 0
13																1 13 0
14																1 14 0
15																1 15 0

Turn over for Parts 3 and 4 ▶

BEC P - L   DP456/356

Photocopiable © UCLES

129

Part 3

16 | | | | | | | | | | | | | | | | | | | | | | | | | | | | | | |

1 16 0

17 | | | | | | | | | | | | | | | | | | | | | | | | | | | | | | |

1 17 0

18 | | | | | | | | | | | | | | | | | | | | | | | | | | | | | | |

1 18 0

19 | | | | | | | | | | | | | | | | | | | | | | | | | | | | | | |

1 19 0

20 | | | | | | | | | | | | | | | | | | | | | | | | | | | | | | |

1 20 0

21 | | | | | | | | | | | | | | | | | | | | | | | | | | | | | | |

1 21 0

22 | | | | | | | | | | | | | | | | | | | | | | | | | | | | | | |

1 22 0

Part 4

23	A	B	C
24	A	B	C
25	A	B	C
26	A	B	C
27	A	B	C
28	A	B	C
29	A	B	C
30	A	B	C

Photocopiable © UCLES

130